Official Discourse

International Library of Sociology

Founded by Karl Mannheim

Editor: John Rex, University of Warwick

Arbor Scientiae
Arbor Vitae

A catalogue of the books available in the **International Library of Sociology** and other series of Social Science books published by Routledge & Kegan Paul will be found at the end of this volume.

Official Discourse

On discourse analysis, government
publications, ideology and the state

Frank Burton and Pat Carlen

Routledge & Kegan Paul

London, Boston and Henley

First published in 1979
by Routledge & Kegan Paul Ltd
39 Store Street, London WC1E 7DD,
Broadway House, Newtown Road,
Henley-on-Thames, Oxon RG9 1EN and
9 Park Street, Boston, Mass. 02108, USA
Photoset in 10 on 12pt Times by
Kelly Typesetting, Bradford-on-Avon, Wiltshire
and printed in Great Britain by
Page Brothers Ltd, Norwich, Norfolk

British Library Cataloguing in Publication Data

Burton, Frank

Official discourse. –(International library
of sociology).
1. Government publications – Social aspects
– Great Britain
2. Great Britain – Government publications
I. Title II. Carlen, Pat
301.16'1   Z2009   79–40783

ISBN 0 7100 0328 5

Contents

Acknowledgments

We would like to thank Mark Cousins, Ronnie Frankenburg, Laurie Taylor and Keith Tribe for reading and commenting on various parts of the manuscripts; and Doreen Thompson at the University of Keele and Ruth Newton at City University for doing such splendid typing for us. A special word of thanks is due to Ian Duncanson who not only generously allowed us to plagiarise his unpublished paper on the Common Law but also allowed us to use it for purposes for which it was certainly not intended.

Frank Burton, City University
Pat Carlen, University of Keele

Prologue

'Pageant of Parliament' by A. P. Herbert
(First printed in Punch, vol. 186, 27 June 1934, p. 708; reprinted in
Mild and Bitter, Doubleday, Doran & Co, 1936 and *Royal Commissions of Inquiry* by H. Clokie and J. Robinson, 1937.)

I saw an old man in the Park;
I asked the old man why
He watched the couples after dark;
He made this strange reply: –

'I am the Royal Commission on Kissing,
Appointed by Gladstone in '74;
The rest of my colleagues are buried or missing;
Our Minutes were lost in the last Great War.
But still I'm a Royal Commission
Which never has made a Report,
And acutely I feel my position,
For it must be a crime (or a tort)
To be such a Royal Commission.
My task I intend to see through,
Though I know, as an old politician,
Not a thing will be done if I do.

'I never can remember how exactly we began,
But I seem to recollect a case about a clergyman;
A mountain was delivered, rather strangely, by a mouse;
There were meetings, there were articles and questions in the
    House;
The necessity for action was clear to everyone,

But the view was very general that nothing could be done,
And the Government courageously decided that the Crown
Should appoint a score of gentlemen to track the trouble down
Which always takes a long, long time.

'We first explored the history of human osculation,
The views of the Mohammedans, the morals of the nation,
And the significance (if any) of existing legislation –
And that took a long, long time.

'Next a little doubt arose about the limits of our reference,
We accordingly approached the Government with deference,
Having ascertained that kisses were of every kind and sort –
Some kisses, for example, being long and others short –
Did the Government expect us to investigate the latter?
The Government replied that it didn't really matter –

'Disraeli was a member, but he very soon resigned;
Lord Arrow died in '98, old Rattle lost his mind;
Still, once a month, in winter, we assembled to discuss;
And then the Boer War broke out, which interrupted us –
And that took a long, long time.

'We then collected evidence, but carefully dismissed
The opinion of anyone who actually kissed;
We summoned social workers from the cities of the North,
Good magistrates from Monmouth, Nonconformists from the
    Forth;
We summoned all the bishops who were over sixty-one
And asked if they were kissed and, if they were, how it was done.
They answered in the negative and said there was abundant
Support for the opinion that the practice was redundant –
And that took a long, long time.

'We next examined doctors with extremely high degrees,
Who thought that osculation was the cause of Bright's Disease,
And one or two Societies existing to suppress
All frivolous activity, including the caress;
Industrial employers said that kissing always tends
To economic conduct and is bad for dividends.
Just then the Great War happened; our proceedings were
    adjourned;

Two members joined the constables and seven were interned.
And I think that it was during that unfortunate campaign
Our Minutes must have vanished – they were never seen again –
For the War took a long, long time.'

1 Official publications:
their historical and constitutional significance

The annual publication output of Her Majesty's Stationery Office runs into approximately thirty million copies. The office keeps 90,000 titles in print of which some 6,500 will be current editions. Its yearly sales are about £2.5 million (Pemberton, 1973: 275). Our analyses concentrate on a tiny fraction of that amount produced by this vast publishing machine. We have analysed committees of inquiry such as Royal Commissions, Departmental Committees and Tribunals or Courts of Inquiry. The subject matter covered by these investigatory committees is arbitrary, they have examined issues as disparate as egg marketing to epilepsy, the control of midges to the workings of the monetary system. In the first twenty-five years of the post-war period there have been over six hundred such inquiries of which a substantial proportion deal with our concern over matters in the administration of law.

The inquiries are *ad hoc* investigative committees that are set up by the prerogative or conventional powers of government ministers, in the case of Royal Commissions nominally by the crown, to investigate and report upon specific matters defined in their terms of reference. Committee members are appointed by ministers, with the help of the civil service departments concerned with the topic of inquiry, and are considered lay experts in the fields of knowledge relevant to the investigation. Cartwright reports (1975: 67) that the Treasury is said to keep a list (referred to as 'The Book of the Great and Good') of suitable candidates who could be called upon for the public service of sitting upon or chairing commissions, tribunals or committees of inquiry. Within these echelons of knowing subjects the judiciary is particularly well represented. Law lords, judges and lawyers are more than twice as

1

likely to be chairmen of investigative committees than any other groups (usually academics and businessmen). In the post-war period more than half the major committees and two-thirds of the Royal Commissions have been chaired by judicial professionals (Cartwright, 1975: 72). In the particular types of inquiry we are exclusively concerned with, those directed towards problems in the administration of justice, this legal presence is considerably higher and gives the reports their quasi-judicial character. Though formally non-judicial some committees might have the authority to mandate witnesses to give evidence and have at their discretion the right to sit in public or in private and to publish or not any minutes of evidence.

The defining characteristics of investigative committees, their expert, public, advisory and *ad hoc* nature, are the grounds upon which their claims to impartiality and disinterestedness are founded. They are formally neither judicial nor administrative but inhabit a consultative space that is technically external to both. This is particularly apposite when the committee is not determining legislative policy but is investigating the activities of state functionaries. However, these colloquia of honorary statesmen, with the help of civil service secretariats, produce reports that receive the states's imprimatur and are ordained as officially recognised discourses. The documents are normally presented to parliament by command, that is they are considered parliamentary publications though produced external to parliament. (There are, broadly, two types of HMSO publications, parliamentary and non-parliamentary, that is, texts produced internally and externally of parliament. All Royal Commissions and most departmental committees and tribunals of inquiry are presented as parliamentary papers. There is no real difference, except prestige and tradition between Royal Commissions and departmental committee inquiries. Also the fact that a text is not a command paper is not necessarily indicative of its importance.) The political relevance of these various inquiries has differed in separate historical periods. The following comments will establish what we take to be their current significance.

The origins of Royal Commissions are founded upon the extension of the royal prerogative to nominate commissioners to inquire into routine problems encountered in the establishment of monarchial power. The Domesday Book, for example, was commissioned by William I to ascertain the facts concerning the ownership of estates, and the extent of population and cultivation for the purposes of taxation at the time of the Norman Conquest. Their use develops during the later middle ages in line with the formation of the royal administration (Clokie and Robinson, 1937: 31). With the institutionalisation of the legal system there developed itinerant justices who provided an infrastructure to carry out judicial, administrative and fiscal functions. These royal administrators were also used on occasions to inquire into allegations of abuse and injustice attributed to local officials and their reports were sometimes used to modify legal codes and practices. Under Henry II one such inquiry investigated the corrupt practices of the sheriffs (The Inquests of Sheriffs, 1176). The Commissioners were authorised to audit and inspect accounts and to take evidence under oath from the baronage and free holders.

Over the next century the rise of the absolutist state is partly institutionalised through the wide extensions of commissions into a disparate number of juridical and economic matters – into mercantile law, the recruitment of armies, church lands, the raising of taxes, the suppression of riots and so on. The period also sees the beginnings of the separation of administrative, fiscal and juridical state functions. The increased jurisdiction of the crown is contested by the provincial magnates, and the rise of parliament at the end of the thirteenth century imposed further statutory limitations on the use of royal power. Under Edward III the House of Commons declared all commissions not authorised by the House illegal and their subsequent use continued for a while subject to formal parliamentary approval. This first era sees Royal Commissions as an integral part of the formation of monarchial administration.

During Tudor and Stuart absolutism it is the privy council and royal commissions that are politically, legally and administratively dominant. Numerous commissions oversee the extension of monarchial authority. Over one hundred and fifty years the absolutist state develops a distinctive political and judicial system which systematically breached common law principles. The royal domination of parliament is challenged under James I by legally informed Puritans and common law judges who contest the rights of royal power to make new law by its own ordinance. Amongst the parliamentary triumphs of the English revolution is the explicit restriction of the royal commission. All commissions which sought to put subjects on oath, impose fines, punish or imprison were made illegal and this effectively curtailed the power of the most important

3

commissions including the ecclesiastical court of the High Commission. In the absolutist period the significance of royal commissions was that of an administrative strategy for bypassing legal processes to establish a form of unlawful jurisdiction.

The association of commissions with despotism and their successful restriction to statutory authority led to a decline in their use in the Hanoverian period (Clokie and Robinson, 1937: 46). Their demise was also connected with the simultaneous growth of parliament's own investigatory bodies (Select Committees), hundreds of which are established in the eighteenth century. Towards the end of the century Departmental Committees come into existence with the emergence of distinctive government departments. This development was contingent on the separation of parliamentary political offices for ministers and administrative permanent offices for civil servants. (See Cartwright, 1975: 35.) From this time the Royal Commissions and the Departmental Committees take on a similar structure and function distinct from the parliamentary select committees.

It is during the first half of the nineteenth century that these public investigatory committees become celebrated modes of inquiry: 'They touched with one hand the ancient machinery of forensic inquiry, with the other hand the new methods of inductive and experimental science' (Cory, 1882: 366). Once again their political relevance shifts, they now become fact-finding and policy-forming bodies, in the absence of a fully competent civil service, during a period of revolutionary social, political and economic dislocation. The concerns, of what is in many ways the Chadwickian era, are to institutionalise new and efficient state apparatuses notwithstanding the prevalence of the doctrine of economic laissez-faire. These apparatuses were to be founded upon empirical knowledge:

> The question of pauperism and poor-law administration, of crime and penal administration, of pestilence and sanitary legislation, and of the evils attendant on excessive manufacturing labour, are conspicuous instances of the effect of commissions of inquiry in reversing every main principle, on almost every assumed chief elementary fact, on which the general public, parliamentary committees, and leading statesmen, were prepared to legislate (Edwin Chadwick, quoted in Clokie and Robinson, 1937: 54).

This knowledge, and its institutionalisation into state practices, was a requirement of the ascendent capitalist class to control the social contradictions produced by an unstable and potentially revolutionary situation.

The model of the new legal and administrative forms advocated by the radical bourgeoisie was founded upon the principles of order, efficiency, cheapness and uniformity that was beginning to characterise the capitalist labour process. The doctrines of Ricardian political economy and Benthamite penology infuse the administrative reformism that is epitomised in Chadwick's remarkable labours. The administrative goal was one of calculated intervention to keep structural contradictions under control so that economic interests could be systematically pursued. Benthamite utilitarian benevolence did not extend to the working and impoverished classes who had neither time nor ability to develop social motives but were doomed to self interest (cf. Parekh, 1974: 13). It was accordingly upon these classes that the hedonistic calculus of utilitarianism had to be imposed by the state through instruction, law, and if necessary, force. Benthamite reformists used administrative techniques to realign the checks and balances of 'public' and 'private' interests. The most extreme formulation of the pain and pleasure calculus is, of course, found in the policy of the poor law commission whose less eligibility principle advocated the creation of a free labour market for able-bodied agricultural proletarians in conditions of mass unemployment.

The factual details upon which legislative and administrative change were to be based were, to a large extent, produced by the proliferation of commissions and committees of inquiry (there were 222 royal commissions held in the period 1800–59). These massively detailed tomes systematically recorded the social and economic conditions appertaining to the colonies, slavery, poor law, urban sanitation, housing and health, the regulation of labour and the formation of the police. Their usage was a strategy in the protracted political struggles that surrounded all the major reforms of the first half of the century. The parliamentary select committees, while carrying out similar functions, were publicly criticised because of their overtly partisan nature, the inexpert quality of their member-ship and their sessional and geographical (Westminster based) limitations. The renaissance of the commission of inquiry met some of these restrictions. Though this is not to imply that they were

5

B

models of disinterested research. The commissions and committees of inquiry were characterised by the extensive use of jobbery in appointments, the packing of committees, the selective marshalling of evidence, the priming of witnesses and the manipulation of public opinions during the period of press release of the reports (see Finer, 1952, 1969). For example the Royal Commission on the Employment of Children in Factories, 1833, was a political expedient to delay the passing of the Ten Hours Bill. Amongst much else it was marked by Chadwick designing a restrictive questionnaire to be delivered by those commissioners he did not trust in an attempt to forestall any prejudicial evidence reaching the minutes. Safe commissioners were, alternatively, given a greater license. Again the 1843 Health of Towns Commission was packed by experts of the same frame of mind as Chadwick. Chadwick himself wrote not only most of the questions but also most of the answers. Similarly the Report of the Municipal Corporations Commission though containing detailed accounts of 285 towns prepared by twenty barristers bears little relationship to this body of work. In fact the draft report was written before any of the town reports had been received (Finer, 1969).

The great inquiries found in the blue books of this period and whose contents are reworked in the writings of subsequent social theorists, eminently in Marx's *Capital*, are clearly products of contemporary political struggles. Their main function was to provide and to publicly propagate knowledge of social conditions that would shape the technology of social engineering. Their contents became part of the discursive armoury of the political scene. As such the inquiries had a clearly dual function of not only creating information but manipulating its popular reception. The Poor Law report, commissioned during a furious crisis over relief, presented a factual and interpretive analysis of relief which together with the calculated release of 15,000 Extracts of Information, created a momentary mood of public panic. The genesis of this and other reports is located within the matrix of conflicts between political parties, administrative apparatuses and the extra-state struggles they are attempting to mediate. The reports of this era are one set of responses to massive social crises through the creation of a pedagogy of reform based on inductive inquiry and public propaganda.

Towards the end of the century their use begins to decline as the executive infrastructure of an expansionist capitalist state is formed. The establishment of a comprehensive civil service with expert functionaries within a devolved division of labour reduced the research role of the inquiries. The technical knowledge required for policy formation became available from state experts and the significance of the commissions and committees changed. Changes in the nature of the capitalist state into the interventionist period have again altered the ideological and political importance of public investigative committees.

The contemporary significance of public investigative committees

One set of popular conceptions about investigatory commissions and committees is jaundiced by a number of cynical arguments. They can be seen as tactical devices to defray government activity, to postpone legislative or other action while simultaneously demonstrating that particular problems are under administrative review and control. On average Royal Commissions take two and a half years and Departmental Committees one and a half years to report and can therefore provide a period where a problem can be held in abeyance. Harold Wilson has quipped that, 'they take minutes and waste years' (quoted in Cartwright, 1975: 211). Moreover the recommendations of a report (when not 'white-washes'), being advisory, can be and frequently are ignored. The potentially inconsequential outcome of a report is not conducive to restoring public confidence. Again, as the research role of these committees should be unnecessary given the development of state professionalism, the reports perform 'merely' rhetorical functions. Such arguments are usually countered in the literature by pointing out those texts that have been influential, have been implemented and were dependent on lay expertise. Their contemporary use, in such debates, is seen either in terms of historical anachronism or in terms of their continuing administrative relevance.

The particular type of investigative committee we are concerned with, those considering problems in the administration of law and public order, we have theorised in a specific manner. We have not been concerned to evaluate the direct legislative and administrative consequence of official texts. The documents are seen as representing a system of intellectual collusion whereby selected, frequently judicial, intelligentsia transmit forms of knowledge into political practices. The effect of this process is to replenish official arguments with both established and novel modes of knowing and

7

forms of reasoning. By linking state functionaries with the lay intelligentsia official discourses on law and order become one part of the constant renewal of hegemonic domination. They are one practice amongst many in the process of reproducing specific ideological social relations. This form of intellectual collusion is a strategy of discursive incorporation through which legitimacy crises are repaired and the reforms they engender are publically presented.

Given this general textual function it is still not possible to determine in advance the content of a report, the actual discourse realised in the publication. These structures of knowledges and reasonings, the official discourse sustained in the text, are a product of the subject, objects, themes and theories created within the discursive regularities of the work. This contention, discussed in Chapters 2 and 3, has limited our analyses to a consideration of the conditions of existence of official discourse and a discursive deconstruction of selected texts. Other questions pertinent to other analyses have not been considered. Conventional criticisms of inquiries couched in terms of objections to the narrowness of their terms of reference, the selection of dependable chairmen, the packing of committees or the dominance of the civil service secretariat (who usually write the first draft) have not been the focus of our inquiry. We read the finished products of official discourses to expose and theorise the modes of argument that can be invoked by a capitalist state based on a formal conception of political democracy during momentary crises.

Different theorists have suggested that the current interventionist phase of the capitalist state by overtly repoliticising economic relations has concomitantly increased the degree of ideological control required for the reproduction of the total social formation (e.g. Habermas, 1976, Hall *et al.*, 1978). Hegemonic and legitimacy crises in the interventionist era represent a phenomenal reaction to the state's inability to control the effects of the economic class struggle during a period of the restructuring of capitalist relations. Hall *et al.* (1978) place the ideological conflict of law and order debates surrounding matters such as pornography, drug-use, student activism, vandalism, racism, football hooliganism and so on, as elements within the hegemonic shifts accompanying changes in British capitalism:

Any profound restructuring of the inner organisation and

8

composition of capitalist relations – such as characterised the long transition from laissez-faire to monopoly, or the more intense section of this are where British capitalism found itself in the post-war period – requires and precipitates a consequent 'recomposition' of the whole social and ideological integument of the social formation. (ibid: 255)

The shifts in hegemonic practices are considered as reactions to forms of crises which result from the restructuring of capitalism into a corporatist structure. The recomposition of British capital has taken the form of increased centralisation, concentration and internationalisation of capital and a consequent revolutionising of the labour process. Corporatist responses to low levels of investment, a slow rate of technological innovation, growing unemployment and a general problem of profitability have produced disparate forms of social contradictions and antagonisms. In very general terms the state reaction towards these conflicts – everything from struggles against statutory incomes policies to transformations in sexual morality – has been to steadily increase the coercive elements of hegenomic control. The period from 1945 to the present, the authors contend, has been one of movement from ideologies of extensive consent to those based more on the 'exceptional' forms of domination based principally on law:

> The mobilisation of legal instruments against labour, political dissent and alternative life styles, all seemed to be aimed at the same general purpose: to bring about by fiat what could no longer be won by consent – the disciplined society . . . The growth of political dissent from the mid-1960's onwards, then the resumption of a more militant form of working class political struggle at the turn of the decade, coupled with the pervasive weakness of the British economic base, have made it impossible, for a time, to manage the crisis politically without an escalation of the use and forms of repressive state power (ibid.: 284, 304)

Within the admittedly broad contours of these developments are located the Reports under analysis. The general hegemonic movement involved has two pertinent effects for this study. The first concerns the increased significance of legitimacy in ideological social relations. The second involves the public transmission of arguments establishing the state's right to coercion. When a variety of contentious issues ranging from picketing to mugging, squatting

9

to football hooliganism are run together to represent an underlying and unifying malaise such as incipient anarchical lawlessness, legitimacy becomes a politicised issue. Appeals during minor social confrontations to the ideology of legality by political parties, moral pressure groups and editorial leaders have as one of their effects the raising of the public scrutiny of the activities of the legal apparatuses. Arguments stressing the rationality of a neutral state safeguarded by just legal codes simultaneously require for their acceptance impartial agencies of surveillance, arbitration and punishment. It is precisely in these periods, where the need for law and order is a political issue, that the activities of legal state functionaries should appear to be beyond ill repute. The ideological evaluation of scandals in the administration of justice will vary according to the specific arguments of hegemonic domination. Accordingly a political cost of emphasising the ideology of legality is to increase the potential damage a legitimacy crisis can create, especially when it originates from the actions of state legal functionaries. All the reports analysed here confront such legitimacy deficits.

Second, arguments based on exhortations for legal or moral rearmament, that are a feature of hegemonic movement, have to be made and transmitted from existent ideological debris. The extension of the law into contentious areas, the alteration of administrative machinery and the changing of modes of enforcement even when directed towards a more punitive or repressive nature still require official justification. The strategies of justification will be more effective, and the legal changes smoother, if they can be made to fit, even tenuously, with established and received notions of law and state. The shift towards repressive strategy is not a shift away from the need for ideological domination, on the contrary its public acceptance is premised upon successfully institutionalising discourses of coercion. The justificatory base for coercive reform is an area of crucial political importance and is one which official discourse is centrally concerned with.

These two dynamics, the significance of state functionaries in legitimacy crises and the argument of reform, coercive or otherwise, during a time of hegemonic transformation specify the institutional genesis of the reports under analysis. Some of the texts are characterised by more of the former, some by more of the latter: all have elements of both in their conditions of existence. The earliest

10

inquiry examined is that of the 'Report of Inquiry by Mr. A. E. James, QC, into the circumstances in which it was possible for Detective Sergeant Harold Gordon Challenor of the Metropolitan Police to continue on duty at a time when he appears to have been affected by the onset of mental illness' (HMSO, 1965, Cmnd 2735). The James report assuages one of the 1963 police corruption scandals (the other occurred in Sheffield) and did much to forestall the demand for an investigation into the Metropolitan police detectives as a whole. Though it was later to transpire that the brick-planting Challenor had also been involved in the police-organised protection rackets in Soho that led to a purge of the Metropolitan CID in the 1970s, the report marshals series of arguments that maintain that Challenor was an 'insane rotten apple' and not the 'tip of an iceberg' (Cox, Shirley and Short, 1977: 11). The subsequent non-public internal inquiries, three since 1969, into police irregularities (taking bribes, planting evidence, acting as *agents provocateurs*, running protection rackets, granting legal immunity in exchange for cars, girls, holidays, home improvements . . .) were to result in the major trials and long prison sentences of top policemen, hundreds of resignations and a restructured CID. Before this James had a wider number of discourses open to him.

The Devlin investigation 'The Report of the Secretary of State for the Home Department of the Departmental Committee of Evidence of Identification in Criminal Cases' (HMSO, 1976, HC 338) confronts the less publicly sensational but equally damaging problem of innocent citizens being wrongfully imprisoned through evidence based overwhelmingly on identification. Though appointed in 1974, as an immediate response to the plight of two relatively unknown victims, the committees reform proposals were released during a period when the 'clamour for change (had) reached a crescendo in the Spring of 1976' (Hain, 1976: 151). This was due to the publicity that the campaigns to free George Davis, the London taxi driver, and to acquit Peter Hain, the then Liberal Party activist, had generated. Devlin seeks to alleviate public disquiet with reforms that remain within the judges' discretion.

A third report is distinctive for the matrix of law and order issues that were raised in the trade union recognition dispute at Grunwick's photographic laboratories. This protracted dispute which brought thousands of trade unionists into a prolonged mass picket dominated the political scene throughout the summer of 1977. A variety of ideological struggles that had been fought out for over a decade – issues about racism, political demonstrations, mass picketing, left wing activism, politicised violence – were crystallised in the minor street battles between workers and police. The confrontation was the most serious industrial conflict the capital had experienced in recent years. The 'Report of a Court of Inquiry under the Rt. Hon. Lord Justice Scarman, O.B.E., into a dispute between Grunwick Processing Laboratories Ltd, and Members of the Association of Professional, Executive, Clerical and Computer Staff' (HMSO, 1977, Cmnd 6922) was a tactic amongst many adopted by the state and other parties to adjudicate the confrontation. It is an exemplary document for demonstrating that the advocacy position of its quasi-judicial findings and recommendations is of a different order to the extra-discursive class struggle it comments upon.

The other two texts are deliberations on events in the war in Northern Ireland. Here the political and hegemonic crisis is of a different magnitude to the legitimacy crises evidenced in the other investigations. The first 'The Report of the Tribunal of Inquiry into Violence and Civil Disturbances in Northern Ireland in 1969' (Chairman Scarman, HMSO, Belfast, 1972b, Cmnd 566) deals with the initial wave of province wide rioting and armed confrontation that took place in the late summer of 1969. The text's origins therefore pre-date the period of the organised struggle against state power which the IRA initiated a year or so later. Accordingly the discursive allocation and absolution of guilt is still designed to restore vestiges of legitimacy. In particular Scarman's legal polish is liberally applied to the tarnished image of the Royal Ulster Constabulary.

The thoroughly repressive Diplock 'Report of the Commission to consider legal procedures to deal with terrorist activities in Northern Ireland' (HMSO, 1972a: Cmnd 5185) is a very different text. The series of fundamental legal changes, such as the abolition of juries, recommended (and later implemented) by the Report represent a reversal of certain established rights of legal citizens in Northern Ireland. Forms of *administrative* internment are reworked into *judicial* due process. It is an instructive text for the manner in which coercive reforms are founded upon claims that seek to root themselves in common law reasoning: to argue that the envisaged changes are necessary evolutionary developments and not fundamental reversals of legal rights.

This book is an analysis of state documents concerning

contemporary problems in the administration of law and the maintence of public order. We have read government writing on law and order by theorising both its external production within the institutional sites of state apparatuses and through the internal discursive regularities of the texts produced. Our concern has been to deconstruct official texts and to expose for analysis the structures of knowledge and modes of knowing realised in state publications while simultaneously theorising their conditions of existence. At a general level the book is an outcome of a theoretical investigation into the connection between knowledge and power relations as evidenced in official discourses.

The particular reports that are deconstructed in our own text are characterised by the similarities of their genesis. All were engendered as responses to specific problems raised by contentious events in the administration of judicious control. These events – incidents of wrongful imprisonment, illegal police activity, mass rioting, confrontation picketing and administrative internment – to varying degrees produced crises in the popular confidence of the impartiality of legal state apparatuses. We designate such interludes as crises of legitimacy and argue that they damage those ideological social relations that reproduce dominant conceptions of the essentially just nature of the politico-judicial structures of the state. Legitimacy is that part of hegemonic domination that specifically refers to state legal structures and practices. Crises in legitimacy can therefore be one expression of a general hegemonic shift where disparate ideological practices are in a state of contestation or they can refer to specific struggles over particular laws, agents of control or administrative procedures.

One established and routine political tactic used in the reparation of fractured images of justice is to hold an 'impartial' inquiry to ascertain the facts of the problem, allocate a quasi-judicial form of culpability and to recommend any institutional reforms that will inhibit future occurrences. It is within these discourses produced by legitimacy crises that the citizen-reader has direct access to the structures of argument that are open to a capitalist state within a formal democratic framework. This book analyses the form, transmission and manipulation of the elements and relations realised in official discourse and theorises this signifying practice as a technology of ideological closure. The function of official statements is primarily to allay, suspend and close off popular doubt through an ideal and discursive appropriation of a material problem. Deconstruction is a reading that re-opens and denies the authorial claims of official closure, a reading that refuses the conflation of the order of the discursive into the order of the non-discursive.

It is apparent that the reports deconstructed in this text confront different substantive issues in immediately differing political circumstances. A report's particular empirical object is not, however, our object of inquiry. We theorise all such texts as confronting, to varying degrees, crises in the administration of justice and we view the texts as objects of the ideological practice of state power. Chapters 2 and 3 argue for a theoretical reading that locates the texts within the state apparatuses while simultaneously establishing the importance of deconstructing the discursive relations realised and produced within the reports. Chapters 4 to 6 consist of the analyses of official discourses in terms of their discursive regularities – not in terms of their chronological origins or external political conditions. Chapter 7 confronts and reviews how we have necessarily had to discuss and formulate some old and still awkward theoretical and epistemological questions raised by the production of our own text. These questions are founded in the following discourse on discourse.

2 Discourse analysis

There is no knowledge without discourse (Jacques Lacan, in
Lemaire, 1977: vii).

Discourse analysis has displaced epistemology. Epistemology's
concern with the roots of knowledge has been superseded by
analyses of the modes of knowing. This displacement has proceeded
(or not) precariously, contradictorily and in non-linear fashion.
Many of the traditional discourses have produced one or more of
the new savants: within philosophy, Gaston Bachelard; within
linguistics, Ferdinand Saussure and Emile Benveniste; within
anthropology, Claude Lévi-Strauss; within literary criticism,
Jacques Derrida; within psychoanalysis, Jacques Lacan; within
Marxism, Louis Althusser and Michel Foucault.

To the works of Foucault we have turned most frequently; not
because these works provide expositions about how discourse
analysis should proceed, but because in reading these discourses,
and in the absence of the analyst, we have been forced to work
within the analytic spaces which have made possible the discursive
knowledge. For that reason we do not attempt expositions of works
which may (or not) have influenced this discourse. Already,
competent critiques 'place' the writings of Foucault and the others.
The aim here is not to drive more nails into the literary coffins of an
Age. Instead, the (unanswered) questions which we pose are posed
within the *bricolage* of the unfinished works of others. They provide
the framework for this chapter.

What is discourse analysis?

> Discourse analysis is a method of seeking in any connected discrete linear material, whether language or language – like, which contains more than one elementary sentence, some global structure characterising the whole discourse (the linear material) or large sections of it. The structure is a pattern of occurrence (i.e. a recurrence) of segments of a discourse relative to each other (Harris, 1963: 7).

Discourse is rooted in desire, a desire to communicate with an other. In language are constituted both the knowing subjects of the discourse (the speaker and his addressee) and (through them) the possible objects of that discourse. Lacan writes (1975: 61):

> The form alone in which language is expressed defines subjectivity. Language says, 'you will go such and such a way, and when you see such and such, you will turn off in such and such a direction.' In other words it refers itself to the discourse of the other.

But this discourse with, and of, the Other is contradictorily directed at capturing future conventionality via an innovatory invocation and denial of past conventions. The extra-discursive desire becomes the discursive necessity. Thus discourse analysis is not directed at discovery of a cause which exists in pristine form beyond the discourse; instead it suggests *why* the discourse takes the form it does. The analyses have as *their* referents only the discursive relations of the texts. Foucault (1972) stresses that, unlike linguistic analysis, discourse analysis attempts continually to be non-normative, to deny privilege to conventionality.

> The question posed by language analysis of some discursive fact or other is always: 'according to what rules has a particular statement been made, and consequently according to what rules could other statements be made.' The description of the events of discourse poses a quite different question: how is it that one particular statement appeared rather than another?

Discourse is therefore not reducible either to the relationships wherein is realised its object (desire) nor to the relationships wherein are engendered its effects (subjects). Foucault does not deny the extra-discursive reality, he only specifies that discourse

16

analysis must give primacy to its theoretical object – discourse. Recognition, for instance, that there are relationships between institutional and discursive sites of authority does not neutralise discursive relations: such recognition enhances and further individualises the discourse by facilitating descriptions of new lacunae, punctuations, erasures and dispersions. Whereas positivistic discourse tried normatively to close an artificially reified 'gap' between reality and language, discourse analysis is committed to permanent obstruction of such closure. The aim is always to *specify* particular relationships and conjunctures rather than to erase them by invocation of an ideal order. According to Foucault (1972: 63–8):

> The determination of the theoretical choices that were actually made is also dependent upon another authority. This authority is characterised first by the *function* that the discourse understudy must carry out in a field of non-discursive practices; . . . this authority also involves *the rules and processes of appropriation* of discourse . . . this authority is characterised by the *possible positions* of desire in relation to discourse. The analysis of this authority must show that neither the relation of the discourse to desire, nor the processes of its appropriation, nor its role among non-discursive practices is extrinsic to its unit, its characterisation, and the laws of its formation.

So, what is the object of discourse analysis?

> A discursive formation will be individualised if one can define the system of formation of the different strategies that are deployed in it; in other words, if one can show how they all derive (in spite of their extreme diversity, and in spite of their dispersion in time) from the same set of relations (ibid., 68).

It is a vindicative triumph of the discourse within which Foucault writes that what is never said is easier said than done.

Discourse analysis – 'bricolage' or bric-à-brac?

The only weakness of 'bricolage' is a total inability to justify itself in its own discourse. The already-there-ness of instruments and of concepts cannot be undone or re-invented. In that sense, the passage from desire to discourse always loses itself in *bricolage*, it builds its castle with debris. . . . In the best of cases, the discourse of *bricolage* can confess itself, confess in itself its desire and its defeat, provoke the thought of the essence and the necessity of the already-there, recognise that the most radical discourse, the most inventive and systematic engineer are surprised and circumvented by a history, a language etc. a *world* . . . from which they borrow their tools . . . (Jacques Derrida, 1976: 138–9).

The purpose of this chapter is to specify the conceptual apparatus within which we read the official publications on law and order. In reading and writing about the government publications we had two main problems; both were concerned with Bachelard's project of replacing the philosophy of 'as if' with the philosophy of 'no' and 'why not?' (Bachelard, 1940). There was the multi-faceted (and continually disappearing) problem of Recognition. If Bachelard had taught us that systems of thought must say 'No' to their own conventions, then how could discourses be read . . . how could a reading be written? There was the problem of Contradiction – a problem which was most present at the moments of its resolution. How could a reading and writing of a discourse deny the possibility of a normative (affirmative) reading without claiming for itself a place of discursive privilege?

Even in posing the questions of Recognition and Contradiction we deferred to the still dominant language of idealist and empiricist epistemologies. In the remainder of this chapter, therefore, we, though necessarily still subject to the logics and languages we dispute, describe the attempts we made to construct a temporary site whence the dominant epistemologies could be confronted and at least *partly* denied their *origins* . . . if not their effects!

Recognition: royal road to ideology and closure? Yes and no

It seems to be generally agreed that the rediscovery of what is familiar, 'recognition' is pleasurable (Freud, 1975: 170).

Truth for the subject is not knowledge but recognition (Lacan, 1966).

Ideology is always a form of the Creation of Recognition (Hirst, 1976b).

Althusser has written that the problem of knowledge is a problem of law (1976: 117). The problem of ideology is a problem concerning rights – a quarrel about rights of possession, a quarrel, initially, between those who claimed a right to occupy a particular place – the space between real-world objects and thought objects. The contenders for this space were locked in constant litigation with each other. They appeared to have nothing in common. They argued over the site of the space, the possible routes to it, and the ways of recognising it when they got there. They even argued over the existence of the court where their claims were to be presented. Yet, upon one thing they were in agreement, they recognised a common enemy, a Pretender to the epistemological site. His name was Ideology. The claimants were powerless to combine against this enemy. They could all name him, but they could never find him. Some claimed that he was already in possession of the site and had to be rooted out, others claimed that he was only a *ghostly* tenant of the site, that although he had a reality, it was a reality which was ghost-like. These latter arguments came to be accepted by more and more epistemologists. And with good reason. For when sought by epistemologists, Ideology always appeared as the ghostly condition of their own existence. When they sought his identity in the mirror of their own denials they could only see themselves. Recognition of what Althusser (1971), following Lacan (1977a) has called the 'Imaginary' (see below) produced a new scientific problem: the problem of saying 'No' to the conditions of existence of existent knowledge. In specifying this problem of the metaphoric and metonymic overlaying and interpenetration of ideology and knowledge some of the parameters of already-known sciences have been redrawn and redistributed in a recognition of their conditional conventionality with each other. This advance, which has transformed the search for the roots of knowledge (epistemology) into an individualisation of the conditions for knowledge, (discourse analysis) has also transformed the problem of ideology into the problem of Recognition.

So, discourse analysis, in displacing epistemology, has also displaced Ideology. But at what price? Maybe, it has been argued by those still writing within epistemological conventions, at the price of science. Even Althusser operated with the traditional binary opposition: Science/Ideology. Yet for Althusser the Science/Ideology opposition is not a Truth/Falsity opposition, it is a political relation between techniques and products (effects). The lived, and already known techniques for knowledge production always already specify the place where science can be known and where, in being known, it is already not knowable. Science has to break the conventions and is known only by its effects which, conventionalised, can be as constitutive of new ideological practices as they can be constitutive of new theoretical (scientific) knowledges. Conceived thus, the Science/Ideology opposition creates a space where conjunctural practices are theorised as having real effects which engender possibilities of both (ideological) reproduction and (scientific) transformation of present knowledges. Such a conception of Science/Ideology also demands individualisation of the practices involved in the production of the discourses. With the individualisation of conjunctural practices which themselves are the products of discursive relations the authors-as-*creators* of the discourse, and the knowing-subjects-as-objects-readers-or-*audience* of the discourse, disappear. Recognition of this loss – a *lack* of conventional unity and a *de-centering* of the knowing subject – engenders the desire which produces further discursive work.

In Official Discourse (as in other discourses) the discursive practices realise forms which have as *their* preconditions modes of lived experience which can be recognised as being either legitimated or non-legitimated representations of the real. We have called the legitimated (recognised) modes of lived experience, 'the Imaginary', the non-legitimated forms we have called, 'the Other'. The (again borrowed) concept which we use to specify the (political) relationships between legitimated and non-legitimated knowledges is the Freudian concept of 'Desire'. The specific usage which we made of these concepts was partly determined by a characterisation of official publications as instances within the Ideological State Apparatuses (see Chapter 3). The discourse of this book is therefore (to some extent) a conjunctural effect of theoretical concerns specified more usually by the discourses of linguistics, psychoanalysis and Marxism. In this discourse the triumvirate of the 'Imaginary', the 'Other' and 'Desire' provides the conceptual apparatus and language which help both to specify the modes of Recognition within Official Discourse *and* to confront the modes of subjectivity made available by the discursive texts. What we could not appropriate were the moments of recognition which made possible the reading of the texts. These moments constitute the (non-author-ised) Other of our own discourse – the loss of the real and never-closed relationship between the techniques and the products.

In the remainder of this section on Recognition we first describe the concepts called 'the Imaginary', 'Other' and 'Desire' and then indicate their metaphoric usage in the analyses of Official Discourse.

The Imaginary

The concept of the 'Imaginary' has been used by Althusser (1971) to describe a mode of knowing which he characterises as 'unscientific' and 'non-theoretical'. He borrowed the term from Jacques Lacan and it is Lacan's usage which we will describe here.

In his analysis of the modes of acquisition of self-consciousness and the unconscious – the latter concurrent with the subject's constitutive insemination of the symbolic order – Lacan describes one such mode as the 'Mirror-Stage', and it is this 'Mirror-Stage' which provides access to the 'Imaginary' (Lacan: 1977a).

The 'Imaginary', torn from the fabulous metaphoric order within which Lacan uses it, can be described as the existential capacity for recognising the specifics of lived experience as constitutive of reproducible self-identities. Recognition of these identities creates and perpetuates the Imaginary order in which the subject lives (cf. G. H. Mead, *Mind, Self and Society*, 1934). This Mirror-Stage, however, which adequately reproduces the 'Imaginary', is overlaid, punctuated and only given meaning by the 'Symbolic', the language which is never at one with the 'Imaginary'. Successful insemination of the Imaginary subject into the symbolic order, therefore, leaves him with a sense of loss, a yearning for the unity of identity pleasurably experienced in the 'Mirror-Stage'. Thereafter the gap between 'Imaginary' and 'Symbolic' is constitutive of a subject who continuously attempts to narrow the gap by ejecting from it the 'Other' (see below) whose presence constitutes both the subject's sense of loss *and* his *raison d'être*. The desire to conquer the 'Other', therefore, results in a 'splitting' of the Imaginary subject who, although effectively constituted by the arbitrary and ever-shifting 'Symbolic' wherein the 'Other' resides, at the same time experiences a lived reality which he 'misrecognises' as his symbolic self. Result: a subject who desires to say 'No' to the 'Other' as a condition of his continued 'Symbolic' existence but who,

21

nevertheless, can only recognise the 'No' of his own existence within a closed 'Imaginary' Order, to which values and differences must be assigned by the 'Symbolic'. At this moment self-knowledge can only come about through maintenance of the gap between 'Imaginary' and 'Symbolic': temporary or permanent closures of the gap condemn both Self and Other to the 'Imaginary' wherein neither can be known. Thus the psychotic who fails to pass the 'mirror-stage' never shares a space with the 'Other' of the 'symbolic' who alone endows him with meaning. The neurotic, by contrast, once *did* share a space with the Other but directed his energies at ousting the 'Other' from the site of their mutual constitution. The resulting neurosis manifests a desire that the space be filled by an 'Imaginary' self who can exist independently and *wholly without* the Other.

In the analyses of the government publications on law and order crises our concern was not the Lacanian concern to describe the subject's insertion into the 'Imaginary' and the 'Symbolic'. We borrowed Lacan's metaphor to describe modes of (official) State insinuation of the legitimated and only modes of knowing. Thus it was a concern with the relations between 'Imaginary', 'Symbolic' and state apparatuses. These relationships, we argue, are determined momentarily by the extra-discursive desire which engenders the discursive project and which has to be assuaged by the discursive practices. The discursive problem of Official Discourse is that it cannot hold up a mirror of legitimation to its own unitary image without recognising the Other (unofficial version of the crisis) which made the official discourse necessary.

The 'Other'

If I have said that the unconscious is the discourse of the Other (with a capital O) it is in order to indicate the beyond in which the recognition of desire is bound up with the desire for recognition.

In other words this other is the Other that even my lie invokes as a guarantor of the truth in which it subsists (Lacan, 1977a: 172).

Expositions of Lacan's thought usually mention that Lacan uses the 'Other' to conceptualise several slightly different, but related, sites of signification. When we used the concept of the 'Other' in the analyses of the government publications we attempted to conceptualise the two significatory dimensions of a discourse to which Lacan refers in the foregoing quotation where 'Other' signifies: (i) *the conditionality of the discourse*: the fusion of the preconditions (desire) which generated the discursive project with the available discursive practices wherein the desire can be assuaged; (ii) *the guarantor of the discourse*: the constant appeal to, and commentary of, a third party (constructed by the discourse) as a guarantor of the truth of the discursive fiats, claims and silences. When analysing official discourses we used 'Other' (as specified above) metaphorically to conceptualise the two following patterns of relationships between 'desire' 'the Imaginary' and 'the Symbolic': (i) the desired synchronisation of 'the Imaginary' discursive practices of official discourse is repeatedly shattered by the Other of the extra-discursive desire which can only be recognised from the site of the symbolic; (ii) 'the Symbolic' which reaffirms 'the Other's existence also denies authority to the 'Imaginary' discursive practices which seek to destroy the Other. Once *authority* (but not *reality*) is denied to the Imaginary discursive practices then the authorial guarantees of knowing intersubjectivity are displaced from the centre of the discursive stage (cf. Derrida) and the reality of the discourse is individualised as the conjunctural relationships between 'Imaginary' 'Symbolic' and 'Desire'.

'Desire'

> Freud reopens the junction between truth and knowledge to the mobility out of which revolutions come. In this respect: that desire becomes bound up with the desire of the Other, but that in this loop lies the desire to know (Lacan, 1977a: 301).

The (infrequent) usage of 'desire' in the following analyses is dependent upon the usage we have made of Lacan's concept of the 'Imaginary'. In specifying our usage of 'Imaginary' we characterised Lacan's metaphoric reference to the 'Mirror-Stage' as a reference to an existential capacity for recognising the specifics of lived-experience as constitutive of reproducible self-identities. But semantic power to know (rather than to reproduce) the lived-experience only occurs with the subject's entry into (and subjection to) the 'Symbolic'. Entry into the 'Symbolic' is achieved at a cost to the subject's 'Imaginary' sense of unified identity. A 'splitting'

23

occurs. Through partial confrontation with the Other the subject knows that his 'Imaginary' consciousness of his lived-experience is only the real but intransitive capacity of his consciousness to reproduce itself as an image without signification. The image is real (effective) but it has no power over the Other. 'Desire', preceeded by an awareness of loss, is thus born of the dilemma which faces the subject who now seeks to repair the 'splitting' from a site which can both *confront* and *control* 'the Other'. Fulfilment of this 'desire' is impossible: to *confront* the Other entry into the 'Symbolic' is an imperative and within the 'Symbolic' the 'Other' is always already dominant. In discourse, the sense of loss which is realised as 'Desire' is the lost (absent) object of the discourse; the object wherein the repressed subject (the signified) effectively but metonymically realises a discourse over which it never has complete authority. A further distinction can be made, the distinction between 'Desire' and 'Demand'. We have just characterised 'desire' (and we do so in the analyses) as the lost (absent) object of the discourse. But the absences in the discourse are also constitutive of the discourse's impossible 'demand' to dominate the 'Other' both *within and without* the 'Symbolic'. In this sense (to quote A. Lemaire, 1977: 163) 'desire always lies both beyond and before demand' i.e. at the moments of its recognition it destroys the conditional lost object of the discursive interrogation. The unfinished 'why not' becomes the already known 'as if'.

As we have already stressed, we have torn Lacan's concepts from the metaphoric structures in which he situates them. The unauthorised usage of them here has been determined by the theoretical needs of a project which seeks to specify and individualise the texts of official publications on law and order – the texts which we have taken as being constitutive of a specific and individualisable Official Discourse. We have called these publications 'official' because they are produced at the command of the government, and we have characterised their institutional site as comprising part of the State's ideological apparatuses (see Chapter 4). But although we considered Althusser's (1971) concept of Ideological State Apparatuses as a useful enough specification of the government publications' institutional site, we did not find his distinction between ideology and science to be particularly relevant to a project which desired to specify the ways in which new (transformative, *politically* effective) discursive knowledge is overlaid and *conditioned by* 'ideological' (technical, reproductive) knowledge. To characterise the reality of a discourse as either theoretical *or* ideological seemed at once to deny the political context (desire) of any discourse's internecine struggles with the Other, and to relegate the Other to that never found, but known-to-be-haunted-house which intrigued (and still intrigues) those empiricist and litigious epistemologists to whom we introduced the reader at the beginning of this chapter.

So we rejected the empiricist conception of knowledge of the epistemologists, and instead engaged in the discursive work which assumed that to know a discourse is to specify the constraints within which signification occurs. Julia Kristeva:

> Semiotics must not be allowed to be a mere application to signifying practices of the linguistic model – or any other model for that matter. Its *raison d'être*, if it is to have one, must consist in its identifying the systematic constraint within each signifying practice (using for that purpose borrowed or original 'models') but above all in going beyond that to specifying just what, within the practice, falls outside the system and characterises the specificity of the practice as such (Kristeva, 1975 in Sebeok, 1975: 49).

Yet our borrowed concepts, although specifying the necessary contradiction between the 'Desire' for the 'Other' and the 'Desire' for the 'Imaginary' did not of themselves enable us to analyse the discourses. The major temptation was constantly to attempt erasure of the contradiction; from some site of epistemological privilege to claim that the contradiction did not really exist; to short-circuit descriptions of conjunctural relations between 'Desire' 'the Imaginary' and the 'Symbolic'. Further, we always feared that at the points of Recognition of Official Discourse's constraints we cast them into the Imaginary of our own 'Desire'. Finally, useful though Lacan's imagery has been to us, we were aware throughout of the problem of implying that the state has an 'unconscious'. We do *not* assume that the state has an 'unconscious' (nor for that matter a phallus!) We only claim that within Official Discourse the state apparatuses, in attempting to repair a legitimation crisis (seeking the unity of the Imaginary), again and again realise a Hegelian conception of the state (see Chapter 3). What we *did* attempt was: (i) to individualise the varying and sometimes opposed epistemologies (paradigms) realised by the discourses; (ii) to individualise the various metonymic devices (syntax) which

25

facilitated the discourse's coherence-in-contradiction i.e. which allowed 'desire' for both the 'Other-of-the-Symbolic' and the self-unity of the 'Imaginary' to be contained in an ever-open space. In our attempt to specify the contradictions *within* their effectivities (and without the epistemologists' irony) we overlaid our own discursive borrowings from Lacan with a *bricolage* of concepts from linguistics.

Contradiction – Why not?

Coherence in contradiction expresses the force of a desire (Derrida in Macksey and Donato, 1970: 248).

The first contradiction then constitutes, as it always does, the first piece of knowledge (Bachelard, 1940: 18).

The transference of the metaphorical apparatus of 'Imaginary', 'Symbolic', 'Other' and 'Desire' to discourse analysis demands different terms to specify the conditions of their discursive insinuations. In the remainder of this section we describe our discursive usage of 'Metaphor' and 'Paradigm', 'Metonymy and Syntax'.

Recent works in linguistics, (usually influenced by the teachings of Ferdinand Saussure) combined with the metaphoric apparatus which Lacan used in the analysis of the 'Mirror-Stage', have not only revealed the instability of the previously held dichotomy, 'science/ideology'. Other dichotomies have been revealed in their empiricist garb. They have dissolved at the edges of discourses which, in thrusting the Cartesian knowing subject from the centre of the discursive stage, in conceptualising language as a process which produces subjects in subjection to chains of signifiers, have also broken through the hold of the 'constraint/creativity' dichotomy, that dichotomy which has bedevilled social science and which, as 'determinism/free-will' has been the dominating dichotomy of philosophical debate.

From the late nineteenth century psychologists and linguists had been investigating the seemingly paradoxical notion that entry into social symbolism is a precondition for individuality. Mead (1934) for instance, used the concept of the Other to describe the acquisition of abstract thought – the ability to go beyond lived-experience. Whorf (1952) put forward his thesis that all conceptual schemes are relative and dependent upon language.

But the dichotomous relation of Self and Society, so dominant in Mead, still lurked within Whorf's work and had been the (mainly silent) 'Other' of Saussure's teaching. For, despite Saussure's emphasis on the arbitrariness of the linguistic sign, the power of signification still resided with a knowing subject. Saussure taught that, 'in each series the speaker knows what he must vary in order to produce the differentiation that fits the desired unit' (Saussure, 1974), and Jonathan Culler notes (regretfully?) that 'it was left to Chomsky to show how the linguistic system could account for sentence formation without denying the freedom of the individual speakers' (Culler, 1976). But Chomsky did not *explain* what he called the 'creativity of language' (Chomsky, 1971 in Searle 1971). His description of a conceptual dichotomy between 'competence' and 'performance', the distinction between the linguistic rules known and available to a speaker (competence) and the use he makes of them (performance) merely reiterated what social savants have observed for centuries – that out of the old comes the new!

In Russia, however, Volosinov had already gone beyond the Whorfian thesis that 'the picture of the universe shifts from tongue to tongue' to emphasising that every discursive act presupposes an addressor and an addressee, and that these addressers and addressees reside within an historical symbolism: 'an addressee is presupposed in the person, so to speak, of a normal representative of the social group to which the speaker belongs' (Volosinov, 1973: 85). It was, moreover, Volosinov's book *Freudianism: A Marxist Critique* (1976) which was most prescient of the Lacanian thesis that the unconscious is structured like a language, of Kristeva's assertion that 'the *major constraint* affecting any social practice lies in the fact that it signifies; i.e. that it is articulated like a language' (Kristeva in Sebeok, 1975: 47). Witness Volosinov:

> the extraverbal situation is far from being merely the external cause of an utterance – it does not operate on the utterance from outside, as if it were a mechanical force. Rather, the situation enters into the utterance an essential constitutive part of the structure of its import (Volosinov, 1976: 100).

Here we are close to a characterisation of non-normative and unpossessed (i.e. non-subjective) meaning. But further conceptual elaboration is needed to pierce the dichotomy of linguistic order/linguistic anarchy. Chomsky tried to solve the problem with his theory of generative grammar, but the knowing subject was still there and still jangling and juggling his bag of rules! Even when confronted the subject still appeals to the rule of law, or rather, in idealist philosophy, the law of rule. Derrida, therefore, stresses the need for a new conceptual imagery; 'When the rule of the game is displaced by the game itself, we must find something other than the word rule' (Derrida in Macksey and Donato, 1970: 267). Lacan's work in linguistics and psychoanalysis provides a discourse within which discourse analysis can be thought *without* the law of rule. By a series of metaphoric and metonymic transpositions, we have been able to use in our analysis of official government publications some of the concepts which Saussure used in his investigations of linguistic signs and which Lacan (equally by a series of metaphoric and metonymic transpositions) used in his teachings on psychoanalysis and his investigations of the Unconscious. From Saussure to Lacan: 'The identity of signifier and signified had to be analysed from elsewhere than a purely natural or purely ideological relation if idealist thought was to be dispensed with' (Coward and Ellis, 1977: 7). From Saussure:

> The linguistic sign is . . . a two-sided psychological entity that can be represented by the drawing:

$$\frac{\text{concept}}{\text{sound-image}}$$

(Saussure, 1974: 66)

In the *Course in General Linguistics* Saussure immediately substitutes 'signified' for 'concept' and 'signifier' for 'sound-image'. Saussure's conceptualisation of the sign can be represented thus:

$$\text{Sign} = \frac{\text{signified}}{\text{signifier}} \quad or \quad \frac{\text{signifier}}{\text{signified}}$$

for it is a basic postulate of Saussurian linguistics that the relationships between signified and signifier are always arbitrary. Meaning is given to words within syntagms which, through differentiation, assign the value of a specific sign. But there is still in Saussure the suggestion of the idealist hermeneutic circle, the suggestion of synchronisations of signifier and signified within the unifying sign. The power to confer value resides with the synchronic signifying chain but, as Lacan (1977: 150) points out, it is still the function of the signifier to 'represent the signified'. By substituting for

Saussure's diagrammatic representation of the linguistic sign a diagram of his own, Lacan demonstrates how to destroy 'the illusion that the signifier answers to the function of representing the signified, or better, that the signifier has to answer for its existence in the name of any signification whatever' (Lacan, 1977a: 150).

Saussure's diagram (as represented by Lacan, 1977a: 151)

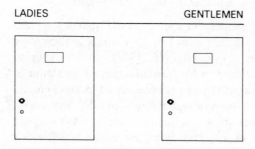

Lacan's diagram (Lacan, 1977a: 171)

And the originality of Lacan's demonstration can best be appraised in his own inimitable style!

> We see that, without greatly extending the scope of the signifier concerned in the experiment, that is by doubling a noun through the mere juxtaposition of two terms whose complementary meanings ought apparently to reinforce each other, a surprise is produced by an unexpected precipitation of an unexpected meaning: the image of twin doors symbolising through the solitary confinement offered Western Man for the satisfaction of his natural needs away from home, the imperative that he seems to share with the great majority of primitive communities by

29

which his public life is subjected to the law of urinary segregation (Lacan, 1977a: 151).

Lemaire is more succinct: 'Lacan's originality is to have wished to furnish proof that the signifier acts separately from its signification and without the subject being aware of it' (Lemaire, 1977: 38).

The 'decentering' of the knowing, creative subject was a necessary pre-requisite for the analyses of discourses in which modes of subjectivity are specified as being the *effects*, rather than the anterior causes, of the discursive practices. In our analyses of government publications the concepts of metaphor and paradigmaticity, and metonymy and syntagmaticity, specify the discursive effectivities of the extra-discursive 'desire' to repair the state's legitimation deficit (see Chapter 3).

Metaphor/paradigmaticity and metonymy/syntagmaticity

In referring to paradigmaticity in the following analyses we are referring to discursive selection from a range of possible alternative utterances (Benveniste, 1971: Giglioli, 1972); in referring to syntagmaticity we are referring to the sequential organisation of discourse, to the fact that utterances are connected in a meaningful way. Paradigmaticity and syntagmaticity are the immediate ecosystemic constituents of a discourse's global structure, the ineffective effectivities of an extra-discursive desire which exists both before and beyond discourse. The *signifiers* (utterances) are transformed, within discourse, into the metaphoric structures which endow the text with its paradigmaticity; the *signified* is an effect of (metonymic) condensation of the pure signifiers, a metonymy which endows the text with its syntagmaticity. Within these signifying practices (and as signifieds) are realised both the knowing subjects of the discourse (the speaker and his addressee) and (through them) the possible objects of that discourse. In the analyses of Official Discourse we use paradigmaticity to refer to both the Imaginary and the Symbolic modes of subjectivity made available by the discursive texts; we use syntagmaticity to specify the syntactic effects engendered by the discursive attempts at appropriation of the Other.

In using metaphor and metonymy to explain the coherent juxtaposition of apparently contradictory paradigms (subjects, modes of knowing, arguments etc.) we can displace the desire for rule-governed unity and, instead of attempting erasure of contradiction we can confront it with the question, Why not? . . . the metonymic question which constantly puts under erasure the reificatory dimensions of the metaphoric As-if. Exploration of the metaphoric and metonymic boundaries of the Why-Not is a prerequisite for maintenance of the space between Imaginary and Symbolic, the space which constantly has to be interrogated if knowledge is to be produced.

Summary

We have used metaphors from psychoanalysis and terms from linguistics to think some of the problems which confronted us when we decided to analyse government reports of inquiries into issues related to the maintenance of public order and the administration of justice. Some of the terms will appear esoteric; the purpose of this chapter has been to explain some of these concepts which have been torn from the conceptual schemes within which they first claimed meaning.

We finally summarise our theoretical assumptions thus:

1 Speakers and writers are made in utterances.

2 They only have limited control over the connotative effects of these utterances i.e. authorship is but *one* connotative effect among many, it is part of a system of signifieds.

3 The linear materials which constitute discourses are themselves constituted by, and do themselves constitute, several overlapping discourses; at the same time they make sense as a very specific discourse.

4 To individualise a specifiable discourse, i.e. to know it, it is necessary to reconstitute (in their absence) the pure signifiers (paradigms) and to identify the syntax (metonymy) which allows meaning to exist beyond the silences of discourse, i.e. at a place where the signifiers are absent.

The readings

The reading of the texts was conceived as an interrogation. The major question, 'Why does the discourse take the form it does?' assumed: (i) that a discourse is a discrete set of statements/knowledges/modes of knowing, that has a specific structure; (ii) that this specific structure can be shown to derive from a set of relationships which have both discursive and extra-discursive forms and effects; (iii) that the discursive effects are realised as subjective effects: author, reader, object, Other and Imaginary. These assumptions were preconditional to the five other, interrelated questions which were posed.

The question of authorship: Who is speaking? In posing the question of authorship we were not asking a question about the technicians who put the reports together, nor about the tribunal chairmen whose names leant authority to a report's final form. Neither the anonymous civil servants who prepared the reports, nor the prestigious persons who gave their name to them were ever authorial candidates. Instead we assumed that authorship is itself a connotative effect of the discourse, that the discourse produces an author, rather than the other way round. The bid for authorship is also a bid for authority; in the name of the Father the Author becomes the Other. But the real gap between author and Other always leaves open the possibility that the text will be given an unauthorised reading, that the author will be read in 'radical ex-centricity to itself' (Lacan, 1977a; 171).

The question of readership: Who can read the text? Just as the question of authorship was not a question about the intents and aspirations of named individuals, so the question of readership is not a question concerning the text's availability or accessibility to a specific audience. Nor is it a question of the text's official constituency i.e. those directly concerned with problems of law and order and who might have a real interest in the report's findings. The question concerns the possibility of a 'correct' reading of the text according to its own directives. And again, it is assumed that a writing/reading produces a writer/reader rather than the other way round. Now the gap between Other and reader constrains the *reading* to be *written* in 'radical ex-centricity to itself'.

The questioning of the object: What is the object of the text? In asking this question we claim at least two meanings for object. The easier meaning is when we refer to the texts' discursive 'work', using 'work' in the same way that Freud refers to dream work. The more difficult (but closely related) usage is when we use it to be synonymous with Lacan's 'demand' i.e. the articulation within discourse of the 'desire' (used by us to refer to political conditions) which always lies before and beyond discourse.

The question of the Other: What makes the object possible? To what silent accusations and in whose name do the official reports reply? The questioning of the Author, the Reader, the Object and the Other is directed at locating the paradigms, the pure (dominant) signifiers. The fifth question, the question of plausibility refers to their metonymic ordering, fracturing and dispersion within the text.

The questioning of plausibility: Who (question of the author) has to say *what* (question of the object) to *whom* (question of the reader) in order to destroy *which* (question of the Other)? Within this signifying chain and as an effect of its metonymic transference of elements from the pure signifiers lies the power of the text: 'It is in the chain of the signifier that the meaning 'insists' but [that] none of its elements 'consists' in the signification of which it is at the moment capable' (Lacan, 1977a: 153). Either the text can effect closure of a problem via a *méconnaissance* which denies the Other, or it can give new meaning to a problem via recognition of a problematic which denies not the Other but the Other's already known conditions of existence. The major argument of this book is that Official Discourse is characterised by a chronic *méconnaissance*, by a continual substitution and displacement of one paradigm by another. This metonymic bid for closure effects the imaginary of Official Discourse.

Investigation of the 'imaginary' of Official Discourse was undertaken as an investigation of the state ideological practices. This last assertion, however, demands discussion. We can perhaps best situate the theme of Chapter 3 by stating, as a conclusion to this chapter, that the major problem in analysing the government publications was to deny them authorship whilst at the same time theorising their institutional site as an effect of the ideological state apparatuses.

3 Official Discourse and state apparatuses

> Writing is the continuation of politics by other means (Sollers, 1974).

> The word is the ideological phenomenon par excellence (Volosinov, 1973).

Official discourses on law and order are products of the articulation of knowledges as power relations. Like all established discourses they are signifying practices that demonstrate the effect of ideology on language: an effect that is inscribed within a particular modality of power. State discourses realise their power in the materialised practices that are called state apparatuses. This text concerns itself with the ideological discursive mechanisms of state legal apparatuses. While the concept of ideological state apparatus suggests the association of knowledge and power relations it cannot in advance theoretically determine the mode, functioning and effect of these relationships within their specific practices. The haste with which analysts rush to forge the links between the apparently externally pre-given forms of power and their internal functioning never succeeds in articulating the precise mechanisms of determination. This chapter wishes to suspend this haste and to illustrate why we came to analyse the texts of Official Discourse in terms of their own modes of signification. We view Official Discourse as the realisation of power in the creation of a distinct object that is fashioned from the discourses of law, epistemology, social science and commonsense. This object functions via its attempts (successful and unsuccessful, and always unfinished) to repair the fractured image of the self-acclaimed essentially just characterisation of the state's repressive and ideological apparatuses. The discourse's conditions of existence, the original site of its desirability, are created by the functioning of the state apparatuses, but the internal form of its signification is the product of the *discursive* relations that realise the object:

> The object of a discourse is established through a positive group of relations; these relations are established between institutions, economic and social processes, behavioural patterns, systems of norms, techniques, types of classification – but these relations are not present in the object, they do not define the internal constitution but only what enables it to appear, to be placed in a field of exteriority (Foucault, 1972: 45).

We are concerned here to provide a descriptive account of the nature of the *desirability* of official discourse, to place the existence of the discourse in its relationship to state practices. This will entail a discussion of the defining characteristics of the contemporary capitalist state and ideological state formations. Official Discourse will be located within the space of its exteriority fashioned by state practices. These practices and their consequences constitute the Other to whom Official Discourse is constantly addressed. This place in which the Other resides does not determine the form of the discourse but, it will be argued, is the condition of its emergence.

The state: its form and functions

The complex loosely structured modalities of power called state apparatuses have not been rigorously theorised either individually or in terms of their relation to each other within the general theory of the contemporary state. While gross and unhelpful distinctions have been made between apparatuses of force ('repressive') and legitimating apparatuses ('ideological') and each category has been assigned specific exemplar institutions (police, military, judiciary, Parties, Trade Unions, media, pedagogies) they have been treated, on the whole, as subject to similar forms and limitations. The general characteristics attributed to state activity will be examined but it will be argued that they do not provide the specific details nor specify the exact causal mechanisms that are required to understand the form and functionings of particular state practices. This contention underlies the significance of studying official discourses on law and order as one form of state power overlapping and unifying the repressive and ideological practices of one state apparatus.

Generalist theories of the state derive from classical Marxist texts that both the form and functions of state practice are given by the structural requirements of valorisation and domination. The state is always, therefore, an instrument of class rule:

> The modern state, no matter what its form, is essentially a capitalist machine, the state of the capitalists, the ideal personification of the total national capital. The more it proceeds to the taking over of the productive forces, the more does it actually become the national capitalist, the more citizens does it exploit. The workers remain wage-workers – proletarians. The capitalist relation is not done away with. It is rather brought to a head (Engels, 1962: 382).

The active mechanics of class power as state power vary according to the causal emphasis given to the processes of valorisation or domination. Either position is essentially economistic in that both render the means of political representation as ultimately determined within economic practice.

The capital logic position   Within the first, capital logic, position the political is deduced as a separate level in the social formation because of the absence of physical force in the process of the extraction of surplus value. However, while the law of capital accumulation dispenses of the need for force in the exploitation process it necessitates a general guarantor of the social relations necessary for the realisation of value. These relations are ideo-logical, legal and political, and are organised by the state. This guarantor is a necessity because the general conditions for the reproduction of the capital relation are not given in the individualist nature of the single capital enterprise. The state functions through various forms, all of which provide the requirements of total social capital: requirements given to it by the systematically inadequate and potentially self-destructive nature of capital accumulation. The form of the interventionist welfare state in the monopoly capitalist phase functions: to provide the general material conditions of the industrial infrastructure, to establish and maintain legal relations, to regulate conflict between wage-labour and capital, to safeguard the expansion of total national capital and so on (Müller and Neusüss, 1978). The democratic form within which these and other functions are realised is subject only to the calculability of effect. For example, from this position, legal relations are expressions of the guaranteed calculations of the contract between labour-power and capital. The public form which law takes, its impersonality and generality, is founded upon the structure of the commodity. The commodity entails both a legal and a monetary currency for the calculation of its circulation. Legal relations are those aspects of production relations that ensure the public enforcement of a private relation. They are the 'neutral' expressions of the system of co-operation between subjects party to the labour contract. Variants of this legal economism either stress that law is an expression of the surface, fetishised, phenomenal form of the commodity or an expression of the fundamental law of value. Either variant derives the legal form (and indeed the state form) from the generalised and calculable mechanisms required by the reproduction of the relationship between capitals and the social relation between capital and labour-power.

From these schematic formulations the state is found to be placed in a space outside of, but determined by, the process of accumulation. Its constant expansion is a calculation of the degree of intervention required into civil society to offset the tendential fall of the rate of profit. State practices in 'late' capitalism are increasingly designed to articulate mechanisms to offset this tendency caused by the increasing organic composition of capital. The very breadth of state intervention into so many areas of economic, political and ideological life is presaged upon the strategies dictated to it by the crisis tendency of capitalism. The most immediate consequence of this view of statisation is to minimise the significance of different forms of state and therefore to conflate various degrees of political repression at the same time as limiting and denying possibilities for reform and struggle.

The generalist-economistic conception of the state can be seen to be accredited with an omniscient feedback mechanism: it knows when and how to intervene in the interests of general capital. The state apparatuses are given a unification and coherence in their global strategy, be it in revolutionising the labour-process, securing overseas markets, institutionalising welfare reforms or monopo-lising research investment, the state is acting as the conscious or unconscious ideal, fictitious, collective capitalist. Once more has teleology found its God and His name is Capital.

37

D

The politicist position Alternatively those generalist theories which stress the state's role in terms of political and ideological domination or hegemony gratuitously extend to the state an autonomy in achieving the extended reproduction of capital as a social relation. The state expresses class power but in a politically autonomous form. The source of this autonomy is again derivable from the structure of the economic mode of production. Within capitalism there is an homology between the relations of property connections and the relations of real appropriation, the capitalist class dominates both. This frees the state from direct interference in the exploitation process and gives it an autonomous space outside of the economic mode of production. The state functions to reproduce and transform the general conditions required by the production relations and achieves this predominantly through political and ideological domination. For example, legal relations make no distinction between property as commodities for private consumption and property as the means of production. Neither does the legal form distinguish agents as owners of labour-power and agents as owners of the productive forces. The form is one of the unitary legal subject which functions to allow both the socialisation of the means of production and the individualised appropriation of surplus value. This absence of class categories within legal and state forms allows the appearance of administrative neutrality. To affect bourgeois domination the state acts as a factor of cohesion between the contradictory interests of civil society. It functions simultaneously to politically disorganise labour and to unify general capital and does so through a neutral, national conception of administrative rationality.

The democratic form of the state is represented in terms of a popular sovereignty that enshrines in the reign of law the rights of citizenship. Political hegemony is maintained not only through the monopolisation of force but also through received representations that state force is ordained by right. Hegemony is partially achieved therefore by the articulation of legal-ideological practices on to politics. Legitimacy, the effect of the ideology of legality on the political, is founded on the fundamental claim of authority that politics is a science inscribed in law.

Given its tasks and its mode of realisation the state is nevertheless accorded a double autonomy. For not only is it 'relatively' autonomous from the class and fractions of capital it also exercises an autonomy over their political representatives within the power bloc. Rather than the laws of capital accumulation immediately determining the limits of state activity, the state is privileged with an intelligence whose operations secure the continuity of the capitalist mode of production. The double autonomy is, however, only a determinacy once removed. The state's knowingness is 'in the last instance' attributable back to the economic. The class based nature of the state fulfils the general structural needs of capital but the space *within* which it operates freely is determined by capitalist production relations.

Poulantzas (1975a, 1975b), in particular, has made use of this privileged space to 'explain' why different historical conditions can produce different types of regimes (parliamentary, republic, monarchistic), with different forms (interventionist, liberal) at different phases of the capitalist mode of production (simple commodity, monopoly). Similarly these differing rhythms and periodisations produce variants within hegemonic practices such as the structure of ideological forms of legitimacy – Lassalism, Trade Unionism, Utopianism. The specific form of domination is materialised within the state apparatuses which are accordingly also sites of class and fraction struggles. It is significant that the relative autonomy causality must see practices both as the effect of class struggles and as the effect of structures. Within the interventionist form of the monopoly capitalist phase the state organises class struggles in the power bloc. It does so in terms of the interests of the hegemonic fraction ('finance capital') but also in terms of the interests of the total social capital. Different types of regimes realise this general function via different forms of legitimacy. The specific problems facing all regimes in the present phase of monopoly capitalism require a displacement of the economic by the political as the structure in dominance. This produces severe contradictions within hegemonic and legitimating practices because they are founded on claims of neutrality and separation from the economic.

Like the first position the relative autonomy argument is ultimately economistic. Both privilege an economic causality that differs only in the form of its realsiation. Both postulate, despite the complexity of the mediating processes of class struggle, a knowingness within the state apparatuses that is ultimately given to it by the logic of capital accumulation. State forms, like other knowing subjects, carry within them only that which is given in predication. Analysis can only rediscover the realisation of the subtle cleverness of this already given process as it appropriates new problems. Struggles that are determined elsewhere are fought out in the political arena and the actual mechanism of political representation do not have a material effect on what is represented. Moreover the ethereal quality with which this economistically given knowingness permeates the state apparatuses robs them of any clearly delineated function. The state apparatuses become defined as anything that contributes to social cohesion.

The variants of economism are not, however, equal. The first variant which attempts to derive the form and function of state activity directly from the structure and process of capital accumulation is clearly, notwithstanding some of its sophistication, a position of economic determinism. The once-removed-super-determinism of the 'politicist' analysis of the state has, however, made it possible, via the concept of relative autonomy, to raise the possible non-correspondence of economic, political and ideological forms. The failure to articulate the precise mechanisms by which contemporary state forms and functions are simultaneously both autonomous of and determined by the structure of economic relations has led to a double determinacy and therefore, an in-determinacy. There are perhaps two immediately apparent ways to approach the exposed lacuna of this residual dogmatism. The first is to embrace a logical relativism of a pluralist causality. Such a position is found in the factorial analyses of the state that characterise the democratic elitist theory of the separation of powers. The other is to invoke a systemic determinacy which stipulates the necessary fulfilment of certain conditions of existence of a particular mode of production or social formation. We shall briefly consider three representatives of this position who are disparate in most other respects.

The new systems determinacy   Hirsch (1978) stands with one foot in this position. He argues that the conscious organisation of social relations is not possible under capitalism, the basic law of accumulation cannot be planned by the political. The laws of reproduction are blind but require (as their conditions of existence) the unimpeded circulation of commodities based on equal exchange together with the free disposal of labour power and already accumulated commodities. The securing of these juridico-political conditions is the state's function, but:

In itself the derivation of objective determinants of the function of the state apparatus from the laws of the reproduction of capital tells us nothing decisive about whether and in what form certain state activities result from those determinants (ibid.: 83).

Rather the form and content of state activity is a matter for class struggle, a struggle that is evident in the loosely linked conglomeration of the state apparatus. This struggle defines state practice as a constant unprincipled muddling through. The state is a reactive response 'to the fundamentally crisis-ridden course of the economic and social processes of reproduction' (ibid.: 97) and is not a practice that is *logically* derivable from those processes.

Habermas goes further. He locates his crisis theory of the state explicitly within systems analysis. The state in advanced capitalism not only carries out the 'steering' imperatives of the economic system (in striving for steady growth, financially regulating the business cycle, creating a foreign trade balance, attempting full employment programmes . . .) but also directly replaces the market mechanism in its goal of creating and improving conditions for capital realisation (through unproductive government expenditure, guiding capital into neglected areas, increasing productivity through training programmes, establishing quasi-political wage settlements . . .). This extensive interventionism re-politicises the production relations in an overt manner that is absent to the liberal competitive phase of capitalism. It raises, too, serious doubts as to whether the state's economic activities are subject to the law of value. The situation whereby the state not only fulfils the traditional general prerequisites of capital but also fills gaps in the market and intervenes in the process of accumulation has altered the relations of production. For example he writes that the state's policy on reflexive labour, labour on labour to improve relative surplus value:

> shows, firstly, that the classical fundamental categories of the theory of value are insufficient for the analyses of governmental policy in education, technology and science. It also shows that it is an *empirical* question whether the new form of production of surplus-value can compensate for the tendential fall in the rate of profit, that is whether it can work against economic crises (Habermas, 1976: 57) (emphasis added).

In contradistinction to the 'dogmatic conceptual strategies' of the state monopolist theorists, who reduce the political to the laws of capital realisation, he demonstrates how economic crises become state-administration rationality, and, in turn, legitimation and motivational crises. This, effectively, is to argue that the conditions of existence of the advanced capitalist economy are predicated upon specific political and ideological relationships being realised in the socio-cultural sphere. Systemic integration requires social integration – in the forms of class compromise, civic privatism, de-politicisation, discursive redeemability and so on. These conditions are not secured in advance.

The final variant within the position of the non-correspondence of economic, ideological and political forms and practices can be found in Hindess (1977), Hindess and Hirst (1977) and Cutler, Hindess, Hirst and Hussain (1977). Their critique derives from undermining the epistemological basis of the causal reductionism inherent in economism. The authors are challenging the possibility of the guarantees of theoretical discourse that are posited by both empiricist and rationalist epistemologies. Both epistemologies invoke the order of the extra discursive, an order of objects external to discourse as the protocols of a discourse's validity. For example, in economic reductionism this can take the form of an empiricist appeal to the facts of self-evident or disguised experience or the form of an expressive teleology of the structural effectivity of a rationalism. To invoke either entails a dogmatist privileging of a causality whose determinacy cannot be demonstrated. To appeal to something outside the discourse as a measure of its correctness (or scientificity) is to conflate the two orders of the logical property of the order of concepts in a discourse with the process of production of a discourse. The evaluation of a theoretical discourse should be arrived at through an examination of the construction of the object within the discourse (the coherence, hierarchy and determinacy of the conceptual ordering) and not through a reduction of the conceptual ordering into the order of connections of social relations specified in terms of the concepts. To do so conflates both the abstract and concrete thought objects with the real objects. Impossible epistemologies have indeterminate effects on substantive discourses. They produce the hiatus between the declared intentions and finished accomplishments of a discourse. It is the effect of an indeterminate epistemology that produces the dogmatic and arbitrary reductionisms that characterise analyses of the state.

It is this critique of epistemology that informs the authors' rejection of reducing political discourses and practices to the effect of economic relations. For the purposes here it results in an insistence on analysing the specific forms of political struggles found within state apparatuses because:

> The order of discourse in the analysis of social relations and the connections between them is not given in the order of social relations themselves: it is a consequence of definite political ideologies and specific political objectives (Cutler *et al.*, 1977: 317).

and again:

> we have argued that connections between social relations, institutions and practices must be conceived not in terms of any relations of determination, 'in the last instance', or otherwise, but rather in terms of conditions of existence. This means that while specific social relations and practices always presuppose definite social conditions of existence, they neither secure those conditions through their own action nor do they determine the form in which they will be secured. Thus, while a set of relations of production can be shown to have definite legal, political and cultural conditions of existence those conditions are no way determined or secured by the action of the economy (ibid.: 314).

The methodological tenet of a non-dogmatic refusal to privilege economic relations leads to a requirement to analyse both the form and content of state ideological practices in their specificity, that is within particular social formations. This residual systems determinacy is one of ineffective effectivity:

> The conditions of existence of relations of production only give the effects necessary to the specification of these relations but they cannot determine the form in which these effects are secured in other social relations and social practices (Hindess and Hirst, 1977: 52).

The three types of discourse on the state that have been referred to have moved from the empiricist causality of an 'economic economism' via the rationalist expressive/structural causality of a 'politicist economism' to the residual systems causality of the arguments of the 'conditions of existence' position. One effect of this new reserved functionalism is to treat all social practices in terms of their internal and ongoing processes of production. For this reason we locate our analysis of the extra-discursive desire, the Other, that is the constant addressee of Official Discourse, within this third position. The Other is the condition of existence of Official Discourse. It is the source of desire that makes Official Discourse both possible as a practice and impossible in its claims. Official Discourse is a state practice which we have analysed in terms of the production of its own internal discursive relations. It is significant to note however that the Other which is the condition of existence of Official Discourse is constructed intra-discursively to act also as Official Discourse's guarantees of validity. To do this, amongst much else, official discourse puts to use the same dogmatist epistemological protocols that have been used in economistic analyses of the state. It is in the structure of the Other to generate images of itself.

Ideological state apparatuses: articulation, positionality and recognition

Through the persistent failure to demonstrate the mechanisms of causal economism, and through a critique of the extra-discursive protocols found in epistemological discourses that seek to justify economism, we arrive at a non-specific systems causality governing ideological and political practices. There are no necessary relations between the conditions of existence of state practices and their actual material productions: there are only desirable ones. There remain, of course, necessary conditions of fulfillment for the reproduction of any established form of practice, economic or otherwise. Within the pedagogic mode of the discourse of state legitimacy we are concerned to examine the manner in which desired relations are realised in official publications, and how desire takes the form of the strategic calculation of political effect. Official Discourse seeks to redeem legitimacy crises by the confrontation and appropriation of unofficial versions of discreditable episodes. To render this Other immaterial the textual formation attempts to discursively appropriate non-official readings. This political calculation of textual effect draws, necessarily, upon existent modes of knowledge and reasoning: both ideological and scientific. What follows is a discussion of the form which these knowledge-as-power relations take in official discourse. It is a form with the paradoxical task of undermining the Other, its extra-discursive conditions of existence, while simultaneously elevating these conditions as guarantors of the discourse's validity.

The general form of appropriation of a problem is to reconstruct the narrative within a discourse that articulates with existent ideological practices. These practices always use science. The textual paradigms and their syntactical formulations are derivations and creative reconstructions of the discourses of law, epistemology, social science and commonsense. The articulation is founded upon the strategic realisation of utilising already established modes of ideological recognition. The text achieves articulation by its activation and manipulation of subjects, objects, themes, statements and theories already founded in other modes of signification. The text functions to creatively re-align the signifiers and signifieds that are the raw materials of its discursive formation. It is through this form of calculation that Official Discourse reproduces representations that claim the state apparatuses are founded upon the general will of citizen-subjects. Official Discourse is a selection of existent modes of reasoning that celebrate dominant normative principles. It is, somewhat like law, the invocation of these principles on to a specific problem.

The primary discursive task is to position forms of the subject. Subjects in discourse are always already in ideology. Official Discourse selects modes of subjectivity to constitute, first, an effective authorial subject (the addressor) and second the addressee subject through whom the text is ideally read:

> Orientation of the word toward the addressee has an extremely high significance. In point of fact, word is a two sided act. It is determined equally by whose word it is and for whom it is meant. As word it is precisely the product of the reciprocal relationship between speaker and listener, addressor and addressee. Each and every word expresses the 'one' in relation to the 'other' (Volosinov, 1973: 86).

Similarly actor-subjects within the text have to be construed as recognisable subjects tailored to specific discursive strategies. Thus the subjects in Official Discourse are so positioned to be recognisable as the same subjects constituted in state and non-state systems of signification. Articulation is achieved by the continuity of the egos formed in Official Discourse with those formed outside. The text's structure functions to achieve this continuity of subjectivity as a form of ideological productivity. In this respect the power language of official discourse is the antimony of poetic language. The latter traverses discourses to create ruptorous inno-

45

vation, the former selects and privileges systems of signification for a creative continuity. It is a process of ideological productivity because the discourse allows movement and novelty without a change of form.

Official Discourse places subjects within sets of knowledges and modes of recognition that produce specific and meaningful readings. Articulation with existing ideological social relations is managed by placing subjects in the discourse within these forms of intelligibility. This is a power relation and is one aspect of the materiality of ideology: 'Ideological practice is doubly material: it works to fix subjects in certain positions in relation to certain fixities of discourse, and it is concretised in certain apparatuses' (Coward and Ellis, 1977: 73).

The ideological practices of Official Discourse place, fix and orient subjects to desired positions. From here the judicious nature of the official publication is expressed in the subsequent interrogation and evaluation of actual subjects' behaviour in terms of the modes of subjectivity celebrated in the texts. These modes of subjectivity use that form of subject already constituted in those signifying practices that elevate knowing, predicating subjects. Official Discourse via this productive utilisation of already established lay and expert knowledges is necessarily oriented to the form of subjectivity that is the *imaginary*.

State discourse uses the language of administrative rationality, normative redeemability and consensual values to indicate itself as functioning within a democratic mode of argument. The state's image as the embodiment of popular sovereignty appears because state discourse reproduces notions of the free choosing discriminating subjects and claims itself as their agency. Within this imaginary form the state becomes the predicate of the collective subject. One answer, then, to Pashukanis's questions:

> why does the dominance of a class not continue to be that which it is – that is to say the subordination in fact of one part of the population to another part? Why does it take on the form of official state domination? Or, which is the same thing, why is not the mechanism of state constraint created as the private mechanism of the dominant class? Why is it disassociated from the dominant class – taking the form of an impersonal mechanism of public authority isolated from society?
> (Pashukanis, quoted in Holloway and Picciotto, 1978: p. 58).

would be that these discourses of legitimacy are achieved through the construction of both collective and citizen subjects in the form of the imaginary.

Official Discourse is theoretically illuminating as it represents the discursive concentration and realignment of dominant notions of constitutive subjectivity. The rules of its discursive formation celebrate the imaginary form of subjectivity. This is so not because the form is necessarily ordained by the extra-discursive (for example by the fetishised phenomenality of the commodity) but is because of the way in which the extra-discursive, the Other, is constructed intra-discursively. In this construction the imaginary is that unified subjectivity whose conscious rationality is institutionalised in state apparatuses. In the discourse the state is given the form of the materialised imaginary of ideal egos. In this discursive claim we have an indication of both the state's desire for official discourse and of its impossible satisfaction. For in the moment of the celebration of the constitutive subject lies the conflation of the intra and extra-discursive, of the ideal image and the material reality. It is this latter, the Other, which has to be constantly excised from Official Discourse but it is also the cause of its desire, the condition of its existence. Hence the flight into the imaginary to escape the Other is impossible. Official discourse tries in vain to abolish discursively the non-discursive.

The mechanics of this process, the enunciative modalities and theoretical strategies, are demonstrated in later chapters in terms of their metaphoric and metonymic devices. They work in conjunction with the positioning of accountable, knowing subjects defined in relation to the Other in the form of an Hegelian imaginary. The object is to unite private, citizen and collective subject:

> The principle of modern states has prodigious strength and depth because it allows the principle of subjectivity to progress to its culmination in the extreme of self-subsistent personal particularity and yet at the same time brings it back to the substantive unity and so maintains this unity in the principle of subjectivity itself (Hegel, 1962: 260).

Gramsci, however, has a different reading about the placing of subjects in relation to political discourses: 'Every relationship of hegemony is a pedagogic relationship' (Gramsci, 1971, 350).

Official Discourse constructs desirably intelligible modes of subjectivity through the rules of its formation. The subject is placed as an effect of discursive practice in a position of knowingness, accountability and therefore is vulnerable to quasi-judicial appropriation. If the subject is the knowing author of his activities the collective subject can judge him in terms of the principles of that subjectivity. This is the construction of an imaginary self-sufficient subjectivity. The desire of the discourse is for reading subjects to recognise the legitimate character of the imaginary construction that is already founded in familial, and reproduced in other ideological discourses. This desire for recognition of the state's miraculous embodiment of essentialised justice is forced to confront what it claims does not exist. There would, however, be no discourse without the absent Other. In seeking to authorise itself the state must confront an Other that for it does not exist. The absent signifier of an Other justice has to be admitted so its existence can be denied. These contradictory moments set the tasks for official discourse: it has to close off those readings which take their discursive legitimations from the Other:

> Legality can create legitimation when, and only when, grounds can be produced to show that certain formal procedures fulfil certain material claims to justice under certain institutional boundary conditions (Habermas, 1976: 99).

> Once their unquestionable character has been destroyed the stabilisation of validity claims can succeed only through discourse (ibid.: 77).

Official Discourse is thus the systemisation of modes of argument that proclaim the state's legal and administrative rationality. The discourse is a necessary requirement for political and ideological hegemony. These hegemonic discourses are a requirement not only to achieve the political incorporation of the dominated classes, their pedagogy also functions to sustain the confidence and knowledge of the hegemonic fractions. State apparatuses cover disparate fields, are loosely co-ordinated and organisationally distinct. Their overall practice constantly and routinely create the effects of crisis because of their contradictory functions of reproducing accummulation and legitimation. The task of inquiries into particular crises is to represent failure as temporary, or no failure at all, and to re-establish the image of administrative and legal coherence and rationality. One of the political desiderata of official discourse is therefore to retain the intellectual confidence of parties, elites and functionaries within the state apparatuses. To create a discourse of unity and cohesion between parties to the power bloc through the production of periodic manifestos demonstrating the state's soveriegn reason. This is, perhaps, a characteristic Gramsci may have had in mind when he wrote, in passing:

> the fact that the State/Government, conceived as autonomous force, should reflect back its prestige upon the class upon which it is based is of the greatest practical and theoretical importance and deserves to be analysed fully if one wants a more realistic conception of the State itself (Gramsci, 1971: 269).

It should now be apparent that just as we accept the limitations of reductionist economistic analyses of the state and political social relations so too do we reject similar analyses of ideological social relations. Ideology is not a falsely conscious representation of reality. A subject's position in the social relations of production does not dictate the representations of the real that he will necessarily have. It is not tenable to analyse the ideological as the falsely distorted representation of real social relations either in the form of one class being subject to the ideological manipulation of another or because of the fetishised phenomenal appearance of reality under capitalism. Either variant dogmatically places certain subjects as epistemologically privileged agents who can know these distortions. It is a view of knowledge of social relations that is a matter of experiential serendipity which different classes stumble across in different modes of production.

Yet criticisms of ideology as the interest-based necessary illusions of social relations have not, similar to the failure of analyses of political relations, managed to excise themselves of a residual economism. Nor have they therefore buried the rationalist epistemological discourse that equates the order of concepts within a discourse with the order of real relations. Althusser's influential writing, for example, has told us that ideology is not a consciousness false or otherwise of reality but an imaginary representation of men's lived relation to their conditions of existence. This is so because 'reality' does not present itself to subjects or subject-classes at all, it is not given off in experience. Rather the subject and his intelligibility is an effect of the social totality whose structures include the 'ideological' as one instance. Neither 'knowledge' or 'ideology' come from the experience of subjects. Ideology is the imaginary mode in which men live their reality. It is the subjectivity constituted for them and within which they live their relation to their conditions of existence. Ideology is the structural formation of subjects in the imaginary through which the genetic fallacy of self-autonomy is achieved. The imaginary is materially embodied in the ideological state apparatuses. The apparatuses are the accumulation of disparate discourses which as social practices effect a constitutive subjectivity. Ultimately the form and content of these discourses of subjectivity is an imaginary mode which functions, through the ideological state apparatuses, to reproduce agents within their places in the social relations of production. Once again a residual economism, via a rationalist conception of discourse, dictates that the modality of representation has no determining effect on what is represented. The product of representation is given outside of its ideological transmission, that is it is dependently reliant upon the economic 'in the last instance'.

As Hirst (1976b) has argued, this position assumes that the economy assures its own conditions of existence and therefore reduces both political and ideological relations to a predetermined mechanism of transmission. In this book we retain something of Althusser's Lacanianism to think the form and effect of the ideological within discourses while rejecting the unspecified mechanisms that retain a latent economism. The ideological is the material effect of those discourses that structure the modes of subjectivity which recognise the desired social relations for the reproduction of a social formation. These ever-changing conditions of existence are not determined in advance by the economic but are the calculated effects of the modes of signification of disparate materialised discourses. This formulation allows an examination of the mechanisms through which such calculation is attempted, in this case through a theorisation of the specific details of the management and transmission of ideological discourses, without a dogmatist invocation of processes external to the discursive formation. The externalities are the conditions of existence of the discourse but they are thereafter discursively constructed. The extra-discursive takes the form of strategic resistances that we define as the Other and which the discourse attempts to annihilate. The confrontation with the Other takes the form of the imaginary. This mode of subjectivity articulates with existent discursive relations in ideological practice. Subjects are actually formed by the structure of the imaginary only in so far as the discursive practice is materialised in ideological relations. This process of the formation

50

of subjects in discourses and practices is one of ongoing resolution and resistance.

Official Discourse within state apparatuses

Of the multiple nexus of discourses realised in economic, political and ideological practice we are concerned with those brought together in state official publications on law and order: Official Discourse. Power is the bringing together of those disparate discursive knowledges so that their materialisation functions to realise tasks within the overall hegemonic and legitimating strategies of the state. Those functions include, first, a technical task of discursive *incorporation*. This process entails the pedagogic application of bodies of knowledge, and the facts they create, into an informational format that is utilisable for strategies of social control. Official Discourse at this level provides a vindication for the implementation of given findings into policy decisions. Second, we are dealing with discourses of *legitimacy*. This function of legitimation sets the discursive task of attempts to repair the state's fractured image of administrative rationality and democratic legality:

> It is to be noted how lapses in the administration of justice make an especially disastrous impression on the public: the hegemonic apparatus is more sensitive in this sector, to which arbitrary actions on the part of the police and political administration may also be referred (Gramsci, 1971: 246).

Official Discourse seeks to dispel arbitrary actions, excesses and lapses to contribute to the maintenance of the passive social control of democratic domination and legal calculation. Third the texts in question provide the arguments and display of hegemonic coherence. They are discourses of *confidence* in which the intellectual celebration of the state's rationality is re-affirmed after problematic interludes. Confronted with constant state expansion and chronic crises the expert discourses found in commissions and tribunals of inquiry are the affirmatory texts that announce the professional functionaries competence. The reports are the exoneration of the system within which the state's men work.

These functions are the discursive effects to be realised within the form of signification we call Official Discourse. The form punctuates existent modalities of ideological discourses, traverses and realigns them to confront the Other that is their condition of existence. The

51

discursive regularities achieve articulation with ideological social relations through innovative usages of the imaginary. It is a mode that places subjects in the discourse in positions of continuity with other ideological social relations. Finally this recognition is managed intra-discursively through the selective paradigmatic and syntactical manipulation of subjects, objects, enunciative styles and thematic choices drawn from the discourses of law, epistemology, social science and commonsense. It is to these discursive practices that the remainder of our text refers. These complex practices realise the Official Discourse of the state apparatuses concerning the administration of justice. These practices are the internal product of the discourse's formation and are irreducibly so.

4 The judicial stare

Common-law, common-sense and epistemology

> Lord Radcliffe summed up what for many is the archetypal
> image of the English judge when he described him as 'objective,
> impartial, erudite and experienced declaimer of the law that is.'
> Perhaps it is these qualities which make judges natural choices to
> chair tribunals of investigation . . . (Lloyd, 1972: 726).

> This chapter's theme was suggested by Louis Althusser's
> juxtaposition of 'law' and 'theory of knowledge' in a footnote to
> some remarks on science in his *Essays in Self-Criticism*. He
> suggests (Althusser 1976: 117) that 'the simple *question* to which
> the "theory of knowledge" replies is still a *question of law*, posed
> in terms of the validity of knowledge'.

When we began this project by reading through some official
reports on law and order issues, we were immediately struck by the
resemblances between the dominant modes of (common-law) legal
reasoning and the dominant (mainly empiricist) theories of
knowledge. Within the texts these paradigmatic modes of knowing
were in constant process of fracture and realignment. Within official
texts which embodied a complex of discourses, the elemental
signifiers were embedded in discursive metonymies which bore
witness to centuries of idealist dominance in law and epistemology.
In this chapter we describe how common law reasoning and empiricist social research are articulated in ideological practice when
judges head official investigations into social situations (crises)
which are characterised by threats to the proclaimed authority of
judicial administration and the maintenance of public order.

53

Common-law discourse

> I do not think it possible to say that a change in the outlook of the
> public, however great, must inevitably be followed by a change
> in the law of this country. The common-law is a historical
> development rather than a logical whole, and the fact that a
> particular doctrine does not logically accord with another or
> others is no ground for its rejection. Best v. Samuel Fox & Co.
> [1952] A.C.716, 727, Lord Porter (Friedmann, 1964: 101;
> Armour and Samuel, 1977).

We might divide the world's legal systems into several different
types. Systems like Moslem and Hindu law have their origins in
religious teachings; other systems, like those of the Soviet Union
and of China are designed to facilitate the construction of a new
social order. English (common) and Roman (civil) law, by contrast,
are pragmatic in origin. They are both based on custom, but the law
of Roman systems is codified and common-law is not. The term
'common-law', however, can be used in at least three not uncon-
nected ways. It may refer, first, to those national legal systems
which are descended from the English system. Second, within any
of those systems, 'common-law' may refer to that law which has
been created by judges who have made new rules while deciding
cases. (These rules are to be found recorded in the law reports, in
contrast to the rules made by the legislature which are to be found in
the statutes of that legislature). This *common-law approach* to
judicial decision-making, supposedly characterised by the rigid and
formal invocation of precedent, may be contrasted to Equity, the
judicial mode which involves a conscious search for fairness in a
particular case.

But what *is* common-law? It has been characterised most frequently by those features which distinguish it from Roman law and
from Equity. We shall initially characterise it by its *method*. When
judges, in their judgments, refer to common-law principles they are
usually referring to a mode of reasoning of which the posited
guarantees are assumptions concerning the evolutionary nature of
the common-law.

Common law has been called 'reasoning by example'. (Bodenheimer, 1969).

It originates in judicial cases, in particular decisions of particular
judges, in accord with the principle of *stare decisis* which requires

consistency and continuity, so that earlier decisions become binding precedent for later cases (Pitkin, 1972).

But the apparent rigidity of the principle of *stare decisis* with its accompanying doctrine of the binding authority of precedent has not resulted in it being a constraint upon judicial innovation. It has merely resulted in the judiciary theorising the judicial space itself as being sited in a place of greater epistemological privilege than that with which Roman law has endowed their continental colleagues.

In Europe the universities have been paramount in developing the law. Common law in its origins owed nothing to the kind of theoretical intellectual approach which one associates with universities. Of course, in both common-law and civil law jurisdictions judicial decisions are important sources of legal change. But common-law originally developed exclusively from them. Typically, in common-law jurisdictions, the judges are few in number, highly paid and very prestigious. Unlike their continental counterparts they do not overtly claim to apply abstract and very general rules to particular situations; instead they claim to mediate justice via a legality of which they are the evolutionary embodiment. But the differing justificatory discourses gloss identical pragmatic practices. Lord Denning knew this:

> [Europeans] adopt a method which they call in English by strange words . . . the 'schematic' and 'teleological' method of interpretation . . . All it means is that the judges do not go by the literal meaning of the words or by the grammatical structure of the sentence . . . they solve the problem by looking at the design and purpose of the legislature. (Lord Denning MR in Buchanan v. Babco 1977 1 All ER 518 at pp. 522.3).

It remains, however, that whereas *de facto* and *de jure* the civil law judge only claims to be a technician, the common-law judge *de facto* and *de jure* claims a rationality which is material in its manifestations and ideal in its genesis. This miracle of common law's pragmatic teleology was well *appreciated* by Coke in the seventeenth century: 'With the aid of logic only how exactly "out of the old fields must come the new corn"' (Coke in *Calvin*'s Case 1608 7 LO Rep 1A) and well *appraised* by Stone in the twentieth century: 'the logic that purports to account for this odd harvest is a series of "categories of illusory reference"' (Stone, 1964). We will argue that the contradictory claims to authority which guarantee common-law systems are logically impossible. They remain, however, as ideologically functional (Barthes, 1977) as the empiricism which characterises the dominant epistemologies of the common-law countries.

All systems of law are faced with the task of not only appropriately applying an abstract principle to a particular situation, but also with the task of plausibly justifying the application of that principle. Aristotle recognised that general rules cannot foresee every specific case and that, if applied rigidly, they can have the reverse effect from the one supposedly intended by the meaning of the abstract principle. Rawls (1955) amongst others (Wittgenstein 1964; Saussure 1974) has explicated the paradox of rule-usage where the antecedent meanings of a rule cannot embrace the justifications given for its application in a new situation. At first sight, therefore, it is often tempting to distinguish between civil and common-law systems by pointing to the seemingly contrasting formalities of logic; civil-law judges appear to argue deductively, common-law judges appear to argue inductively. It is not as simple as that.

Every civil-law country has a code or codes containing principles of law at a fairly high level of generality. The connotative gaps between abstract statements, their concrete application, and their effective meanings in a judicial decision, allow the creation of new law to suit (or not) social, economic or political conditions not foreseen by those who drafted the codes. Individual civil-law statutes, too, may be more general in their wording than those with which English judges are happy. English statutes, instead of setting out general aims and principles to guide officials in the task of implementation, are attempts at precise instructions.

But the general principles of English law are not to be found in the statute book. They are contained in the vast mass of decided cases, including the growing number of National Insurance Commissioners' Decisions, which are referred to not by names but by numbers. This feature of the common-law has led some commentators to argue that, 'in studying the common-law, it is often difficult to be sure just which features of a case were the decisive ones . . .' (Pitkin, 1972). But the same difficulty is encountered by students of civil law. To believe that the principles of deductive logic always operate in one system (the civil law) and that those of inductive logic operate in the other (common-law) would indeed be to collude in their overt self-characterisations; it would not provide much knowledge of the specifics of common-law judicial practices. The frequent observations about the common-law's apparently paradoxical rigidity and flexibility get closer to its essence. Thus Pitkin (1972: 51) adequately portrays the distinctive features of common-law:

> Of course, common-law courts do write opinions and are expected to be consistent, so principles of common-law do exist also. *But the way those principles are articulated, and used, and learned, is different from the way the precepts of Roman-law are articulated, used and learned.* The articulation of principles by a common-law court, like the Court's statement about which features of a case were decisive, is always subject to further articulation and revision in later cases, in ways that could not have been foreseen [our emphasis].

We are arguing that what is striking about the common-law, a system which above all else rhetorically celebrates the principle of *stare decisis* and the doctrine of precedent, is the mode of its justificatory (legitimacy-seeking) logic. Unlike some other commentators we do not see its paradoxical claims to both rigidity and flexibility as being merely a celebration of liberalism. Instead we theorise its mode of resolution of apparent paradox as an instrumental mode which makes the common-law as politically flexible as it is epistemologically absurd (for examples, see Sachs, 1976; Spicer, 1976). Common-law constitutes a discourse embedded in, and made possible by, forms of reasoning which always deny, and ultimately destroy, their own epistemologies. In Chapter 5 we will indicate how judicial appeals to common-law reasoning presuppose the same guarantees as do appeals to common-sense and how the effectivity of such appeals contradict their epistemological connotations.

Common-sense

> What we need is unimpeachable authority for the fundamental convictions shared by all normal men about matters of fact with respect to which consciousness can give no guarantee (Grave, 1967 on Berkeley).

> I think that I have solved a major philosophical problem: the

problem of induction. (I must have reached the solution in 1927 or thereabouts) (Popper, 1972).

I was able, with two superb Northern Irish colleagues, to destroy myth and legend and to make it more difficult for prejudice to arise in the future (Lord Scarman (1976) talking about his Northern-Ireland enquiry).

The concept of common-sense has been accredited with several meanings, but its employment has usually been directed at asserting the existence of sets of knowledges, and ways of knowing, which are equally available (in greater or lesser degree) to all human beings. The various definitions of common-sense which are given in the *Encyclopaedia of Philosophy* and the *New English Dictionary* all assert the determinative nature of rules in a rule-governed world. When common-sense is invoked in common-law discourse, however, normality and rationality are tacitly presented as being the ideal representations of specific conjuctures, the mediation of which, it is claimed, is the monopoly of professional pedagogues. But common-law, like common-sense, 'does not declare itself in advance of an attack upon it' (Grave 1967). Writers on common-law have always known this: 'There are usually plenty of precedents to go around; and with the accumulation of decisions, it is no great problem for the lawyer to find legal authority for most decisions' (Douglas, 1964). And legal authority, like common-sense, can claim to be at one with the conditions of its existence. Thus, Mr Justice Cardozo:

However colloquial and uncertain the words had been in the beginning, they had won for themselves finally an acceptance and a definitiveness that made them fit to play a part in the legislative process. They came into a statute . . . freighted with the meaning imparted to them by the mischief to be remedied and by contemporaneous discussion . . . In such conditions history [as embodied in Mr Justice Cardozo] is a teacher that is not to be ignored. Duparquet Co. v. Evans, 297, U.S. 216, 220, 221 (1936) quoted in Frankfurter (1964: 52).

This is what common-law reasoning, common-sense and epistemology have always had in common: an effective recognition of the constantly changing material conditions which make their contradictory claims possible. A brief consideration of the ways in which three common-sense theorists, Hume, Durkheim and Popper, conceive of their epistemological/moral problems will indicate that the plasticity inherent in empiricism's appeals to common-sense provides the blueprint for the sophistications (and successes) of common-law rhetoric.

David Hume's empiricist philosophy was based on the familiar idealist distinctions between appearances and ideas, between passion and reason. According to Hume, all claims to knowledge are based on sensory experiences of nature. On the bases of sensory experiences claims can be made about the appearances of things, but inductive logic cannot be used to produce knowledge about the nature of things as represented by ideas. Yet, said Hume, unless we did use inductive logic to make assumptions about the nature of things we could hardly make any practical decisions at all. Thus did Hume invoke common-sense to nullify his rationalist critique of empiricism. Exit Hume.

Emile Durkheim's sociology is liberally sprinkled with claims concerning the distinction between common-sense and science. Like Hume's scepticism, Durkheim's scepticism is the product of a moralistic quest for social salvation through rules. Both Hume and Durkheim thought that societies could be known subjectively through their manifestations and objectively through their products (Parsons, 1937), though, as Parsons points out, according to such a logic, the posited social reality could itself never be known. Further, as Durkheim's sociology rested on two basic concepts of Individual and Society, it followed that he had to pose the question of the relationship between the two. The answer was always the same: the determinate relationship was normative. Such an answer, parallel to that usually given in answer to the recurring questions concerning the determinate relationships between individuals and the law, had to involve a psychology of the individual. This is a constant feature of common-sense reasoning: there always comes a point when the knowing subjects, whose posited common-sense makes empiricism possible, have to be transformed into the *hierarchy of knowing subjects* whose privileged (or not) common-sense, makes official adjudication possible. So, in his *Professional Ethics and Civic Morals* Durkheim entrusted to professional groups the correct (moral) interpretation of social rules. Then, at the end of this book, Durkheim's scepticism came full circle and, lamenting the unknowability of the relationship between Individual and Society, Durkheim put his faith not in science but in 'human love'. Exit Durkheim, enter Humanism.

Karl Popper asserts that he solved the problem of induction in 1927. He remains, however, a great admirer of common-sense. According to Popper, common-sense has two faces, the one discovered by Hume, which Popper dismisses as absurd, and the one discovered by Popper which, according to Popper, would also be absurd if utilised as an epistemology, but which, as *ontology* can be converted into realism without relapsing into Hume's idealism. In plotting the three stages by which Popper's realism is converted by his own usage of common-sense into Hume's idealism, we shall also be indicating how Popper's sophisticated arguments exactly parallel judicial pronouncements about the common law.

Popper's starting point is his claim that there is an objective knowledge which is human knowledge. Such knowledge is not only created by humans but emanates from the complex workings of human organisms at certain stages of development. (Re-enter Human-Nature, cross-fertilised by Kant and Darwin). This knowledge is evolutionary. It grows! (Enter developmental psychology). Finally, this human knowledge is self-correcting, its 'auto-correctionalism' being dependent upon the 'common-sense' knowledge of a 'healthy organism'. (Enter, upon cue, the judiciary!)

The three 'common' sense theorists whose works we have mentioned were quite open in their aims. Each of them (like the common-law judge) was concerned with the preservation of the posited moral and intellectual values of an Age. Having pessimistic views of human-nature both Durkheim and Popper thought that it could be favourably developed only by an epistemologically-privileged group who would fashion sets of rules, i.e. a social technology, capable of distinguishing between true and false beliefs about the world. Neither of them, however, believed that such a technology could be developed. The essential imperfectability of Mankind pre-empted the possibility of Truth, but an image of knowledge could be *created*; through the clever manipulation of rules an object could be presented that was truth-like. One could, as Popper claimed, create verisimilitude. Verisimilitude, the product of the professional adjudicator, would also have a guarantee . . . common-sense.

When Hume's philosophical scepticism had failed in the eighteenth century God was still around and Hume, in despair of epistemology, had finally located the guarantees of human knowledge in His wisdom. Durkheim had available to him that more modern refuge for common-sense sceptics – Humanism. But for

Popper there is verisimilitude, the common-sense which is always at one with the conditions of its existence. For, like the common-law, verisimilitude is ultimately located in that unknowable space between mind (or individual) and nature (or society). It is to be apprehended through rules which decide the degree of correspondence between the theory (or abstract concept) and the real world. The fit between this unknowable 'real world' and the rules which mediate it is guaranteed by the superior techniques available to those whose training (scientific or legal) increases their innate human aptitude for reproducing already-known representations of the ideal. In conflating the medium and the message, common-sense theorists, like legal positivists, accurately describe the imaginary, but in a mode by which it (like Durkheim's society or Popper's verisimilitude) can never be known. It is because they can never be known that both common-sense and common-law are, as we have already noted 'always subject to further articulation and revision . . . in ways that could not have been foreseen' (Pitkin, 1972: 51).

In even the briefest attempt at prising apart some of the hermetic discourses which have dominated the writings of three influential social philosophers of the eighteenth, nineteenth and twentieth centuries we have shown how common-sense, despite the multiplicity of its philosophic guises, repeatedly nullifies its own claims to coherence through contradictory assumptions of: epistemological guarantees/epistemological agnosticism; privileged knowing-subjects/democratic humanism; separation of subject and object/conflation of subject and object; eternal truth/evolutionary truth. Yet, despite its logical contradictions, and as Marxist writers have repeatedly pointed out, common-sense has both discursive effects and ideological effectivity, i.e. it becomes metonymically sedimented in totally disparate discourses. Engels, for instance, in *Anti-Duhring*, deals at length with common-sense as the eternal truth which cements morality and law; modern examples of such common-sense jurisprudence can be seen in the work of Twining and Miers (1976) and Rawls (1972) – to name but two of the worst examples.

Although in *The German Ideology* Marx and Engels opposed the rational-idealist (Kantian) and rational-speculative (Hegelian) critiques of common-sense reasoning with a rational materialist exposition of the distinction between appearance and reality, in the first volume of *Capital* Marx is more concerned to demonstrate both *why* bourgeois thought takes the form it does and *why* it has real effects e.g. 'The categories of bourgeois economy . . . are forms of thought expressing with social validity the conditions and relations of a definite, historically-determined mode of production' (Marx, 1967: 76). And it hardly needs to be said that discursive attack is a central element in Marx's theoretical practice: 'These mental developments . . . take root and have to be combatted' (Marx, ibid.). Further it is common-sense as ideological *practice* rather than common-sense as 'non-truth' 'distortion' 'myth' or 'class-bound interest' which has to be combatted. As Gramsci (1971: 423) has commented:

> References to common-sense and to the solidity of its beliefs are frequent in Marx. But Marx is referring not to the validity of the content of these beliefs but rather to their formal solidity and to the consequent imperative character they have when they produce norms of conduct.

Gramsci too, although concerned with the usual and recurring themes of common-sense's incoherence, fragmentation and elitism, is also concerned with going beyond rational-materialist critique. In a passage prescient of Foucault's writings on discourse analysis Gramsci outlines the strategy for mounting a discursive and non-epistemological attack on common-sense:

> What must be explained is how it happens in all periods there co-exist many systems and currents of philosophical thought, how these currents are born, how they are diffused and why in the process of diffusion they fracture along certain lines and in certain directions (Gramsci, 1971: 327).

It is as one element of such discursive work that in this chapter we are indexing some of the *judicial* modes of articulation of common-law, common-sense and epistemology.

Epistemology

> The function of articulated judicial reasoning is to help protect the courts' power by giving some assurance that private views are not masquerading behind public view (Levi, in Hook, 1964: 281).

Within the discursive practices of the common-law mode are embedded structures of argument that seek to celebrate their own adjudications. These arguments have as *their* court of appeal variants of the classical epistemologies. We shall argue that though common-law discourse is neither produced nor internally ordered by theories of knowledge, it attempts to legitimise its discursive practices by appeals to the language of prescriptive methodology. Common-law reasonings's assertive self-confidence is projected through the guaranteed claims implicit in its invocation of epistemological discourses. In illustrating the mechanics of this process we shall argue that the discursive legitimations of the common-law mode are entirely pragmatic and its guarantees vacuous and incoherent.

The theory of knowledge evidence in the courts is eclectic. It is primarily empiricist in its elevation of the facts of experience as the arbiter in determining the correct decision. Yet in its insistence on the normative character of the law, the common-law invokes a rationalist method to decide which principle, which legal concept, is to be applied to particular cases. The constant juggling between legal experience and legal reason produces the pragmatist circle of the common-law mode. The doctrine of *stare decisis* (standing by past decisions) requires applying the law 'as it is'. This given object, the law as it is, becomes embodied in the *ratio decidendi* (the reason for the decision) of past causes. How is it known which principle of reason is to apply to instant and future cases? The facts of the case guide us. But what facts of the case are relevant? This involves invoking past principles. . . . Within the space created by this epistemological conundrum is fashioned the site of the judicial agent. Mediating the decisionism entailed in the correct selection of relevant facts and principles is the knowing subject of both rationalist and empiricist epistemologies: the janus-faced judge, at once judge of judicial and epistemological discourse, the guardian of the evolutionary unfolding of verisimilitude.

Empiricism

> To follow past decisions is a natural and indeed a necessary
> procedure in our everyday affairs. To take the same course as has
> been taken previously, or as has usually been adopted in the past,
> not only confers the advantage of the past but also saves the
> effort of having to think out a problem anew each time it arises
> (Lloyd, 1972: 702).

In such a manner does jurisprudence, the discourse on legal

discourse, typically introduce *stare decisis*. Judicial discourse, in its celebration of the accumulated experience of thousands of court decisions, appeals to the ideality of historical continuity and legal certainty. The facts of legal experience become the chief referee in the adjudication of single cases. These facts of experience become established principles, universal legal statements. They become the inductively arrived-at abstractions that serve as benchmarks for particular cases.

Though Popper would see his deductive nomological empiricism as radically different to this classical inductivism, the resemblances with the common law mode are more than superficial. The body of precedent act as universal statements from which a current case can be deduced. Popper's universal statements appear as the products of rational criticism, theories which have an empirical content as yet un-refuted. Common-law precedent is, however, unashamedly normative. Yet Popper's resistance to the notion of an atheoretical observational language in which universal statements can be tested and his insistence on the theoretical content of all observation introduces a normative element into his methodology. If observation is theoretically impregnated then the claims of competing theories cannot be logically preferred in terms of their empirical contents. In place of the logic of empirical guarantees Popper puts forward a conventionalist position. The refutation of a universal statement is ultimately a matter of decision. He maintains that this decisionism is rational because in the absence of any certain mechanism for the adjudication of competing and non-competing theories we are forced to decide. The criterion for guiding such decisions are locked into the pedagogic experience of the scientific community: bold conjectures, constant critical attack, empirical refutation, third world relations and a linguistically based correspondence theory of truth. These as Williams (1975) remarks are institutional controls on the knowing subject of the scientific community. These controls necessitate decisions which are ultimately normative. But decisionism is not therefore arbitrary: scientific norms are epistemologically privileged, perhaps similar to legal norms?

That it does not [convention imply arbitrariness] should have been clear from my example of the jury, which plays such a role in Logik de Forschung, section 30. The jury decides about a fact – say whether Mr A killed Mr B. Its decision is the result of prolonged deliberation; much time is needed for coming to a common decision (which is the meaning of 'convention' intended here). But who would say that a jury which has long and seriously debated the issue decides 'completely arbitrarily'? Its decision is the result of a common effort to *find the truth*.

From a purely logical point of view, its decision may be called 'arbitrary' in so far as the accepted statement [the verdict] is in no way logically derivable from any other [given statement]. . . .

So it is too with scientific hypotheses . . . 'the acceptance or rejection of them is a matter for something like a scientific jury – the scientific community (which may or may not come to an agreement)' (Popper, 1974: 1111). It was Kuhn's insistence that such juridical conventionalism may not be entirely rational that was to expose the essential dogmatism of falsificationism. In Kuhn the history of science is ordered to illustrate that the pedagogic experience of scientists has an element of socialisation into a theoretical world-view. This paradigm structures the nature of the theoretical and empirical problems that are posed within science, it is not a guarantee of the logic of discovery or validity but: 'Instead, like an accepted judicial decision in common-law, it is an object for further articulation and specification under new or more stringent conditions' (Kuhn, 1970: 23).

Rationalism The incoherence that the prescriptive epistemology of scientific method faces when confronted with the indeterminate consequences of the doctrine of decisionism (Lakatos, 1970; Feyerabend, 1975) leaves judicial discourse unabashed. This is because judicial discourse also elevates the normative content of legal concepts. The facts of past experience dominate common-law reasoning but it is recognised that the factual cannot speak for itself and requires structuring through normative principles. The law as a system of normative rationalism invokes an alternative order of justification and a different language of validity:

a particular form of use of language, different from that part of language concerned with propositions of fact, but it is a no less legitimate usage than factual statements, and, is, indeed, related to a whole group of similar 'normative' usages such as commands, exhortation, and moral, ethical, or religious codes or rules of conducts (Lloyd, 1972: 8).

The articulation of precedent on to future cases requires the clarification of the normative principles of the law. These are the *ratio decidendi* which contribute to the rational ordering of common-law adjudication and carry its essence. The normative values embodied in common-law are not arbitrary, they arise initially from accumulated experience and practice and are then internally structured to minimise contradiction. Experience and reason combine, the facts of the past become the principles of the present. Within these two criteria for adjudicative decisionism is created the space for the judicial agent. Each case requires a creative appraisal of which facts and what principles are relevant to the litigation. On the one hand *stare decisis* must not be applied too rigidly less it breach legal principles: 'A rigid doctrine is inimical to the scientific development of the law, since bad decisions stand out like signposts directing the law into wrong paths and so impeding a rational approach' (Lloyd, 1972: 715).

> When these ghosts of the past stand in the path of justice clanking their medieval chains the proper course for the judge is to pass through them undeterred (Lord Denning MR, Letang v. Cooper (1905) QB 232 Court of Appeal).

Yet on the other hand these principles of justice are not always clear, there may be more than one *ratio decidendi* capable of being invoked:

> It is in choosing between such alternative principles that the interest shifts to the elements of technique, skill, experience and plain wisdom with which such choices are made. It may be added that these are the matters upon which Llewellyn places stress in his book The Common Law Tradition, where he notes no less than sixty-four techniques for handling precedent (Lloyd, 1972: 719).

So it is that the judge who ostensibly only applies the law as it is, is privileged to puncture the tautology of the reason/experience couple. The consequence of this justificationism is pragmatic instrumentalism:

> The courts will inevitably approach different cases in different ways, some with greater and some with a less measure of freedom. It is this freedom to manoevre which is really enshrined

in the traditional theory. For though that theory may appear to place undue stress upon the actual formulation of the rule by the original court, it is qualified by the need for later courts to decide how far that formulation was or was not 'necessary' for the purposes of the decision. For this purpose the later courts will scrutinise both the facts of the earlier case, as far as these appear in the judgement or elsewhere, and the language of the judge. In interpreting these the later court is likely to be influenced by many variable factors, such as the age of the earlier case; who were the judges composing the court; the arguments which were put forward and examined by it; and its own sense of the needs of the situation and how far it is felt desirable to extend or limit the express formulation of that earlier decision (Lloyd 1972: 720–1).

The pragmatic space situated by the justices is the space of the indeterminate consequences of judicial epistemology. The judicial discourse of the common-law seeks its legitimation through its appeal to the classical guarantees of validity. This legitimation fashions a discursive lacuna within which judicial discourse determines its own concepts, its own subjects, objects, themes and theories.

Hindess (1977) and Hindess and Hirst (1977) have argued that the process of the production of a discourse must be separated from the logical order of the concepts of a discourse. This prescription emerges from their contention that epistemology is dogmatic in its structure and indeterminate in its effects on substantive discourses. Both empiricist and rationalist epistemologies prescribe protocols which depend upon theorising knowledge as a distinction and a correlation between a knowing subject and a known real object. Both deal with objects given to them and conflate this given object with the object constituted by discursive relations, the thought-object. The claims of epistemology to evaluate discourses on the grounds of extra-discursive methodological prescriptions involves privileging objects outside of the discourse as measures of intra-discursive validity. In empiricist epistemology knowledge results from a distinction and correlation between concepts and observations through the setting up of correspondence rules by which concepts are operationally defined. These correspondence rules are mediated through the agency of the experience and judgment of the human subject to produce the privileged order of the factual.

In rationalist epistemology reality is theorised as a rational order whose parts and relations correspond to concepts and their relations: 'Rationalism claims to reproduce the real in the form of abstraction through the order of discourse' (Hindess and Hirst, 1977: 13). The order of extra-discursive privilege is the categorical or conceptual which makes the discourse possible and which corresponds to the essence of the real object.

It is the privileging of levels that reveals epistemological doctrine as dogma: 'An epistemology is a dogmatism in the sense that it posits a certain level or form of discourse as being epistemologically privileged and ultimately immune to further evaluation' (Hindess and Hirst, 1977: 21). It is the establishment by fiat of extra-discursive levels (the factual, the conceptual) as the adjudicators of discourses which demonstrates the arbitrary nature of classical epistemology. Hindess extends the consequences of the argument: if epistemology is arbitrary and incoherent in its prescriptions then it is also indeterminate in its effect on substantive discourses (Hindess, 1977: 219.20). The practical consequence of this argument is that a critique of epistemology cannot be extended into a critique of any particular discourse. That evaluation takes place in terms of the consistency, coherence and determinate nature of the order of concepts and their relations within a discourse.

We have not, therefore, sought the appraisal of judicial discourse in terms of its epistemological legitimations. This chapter has involved an analysis of the jurisprudential gloss that the discourse of the common-law appeals to. These epistemologies alone do not make the discourse possible nor does an exposure of their inconsistencies make the discourse incoherent. What these epistemological glosses do is to constitute an ideal discourse through which the common-law discourse seeks legitimation. The material discourse of the common-law uses epistemologies as justificatory appendages, The exposure of the eclectic manner in which rationalist and empiricist method is involved in jurisprudence does not render the common-law incoherent for its coherence has a material existence. But the exposure of its 'fetishist' form does point to the instrumental and materialistic nature of judicial discourse. It is precisely in the deconstruction of the justificatory arguments which necessitate the judicial agent that we can establish the essentially materialistic character of judicial discourse. Behind the judicial stare is the force of a political desire.

5 The judicial discourse

And when the Legislator (he who claims to lay down the Law) presents himself to fill the gap, he does so as an imposter (Lacan, 1977a: 311).

The *judicial stare* describes the ideological site where common-law, common-sense and epistemology are conflated. In this chapter we deconstruct two official reports. First we describe how the judicial stares becomes a precondition for adjudicative narrative with its hierarchy of knowing subjects. Second we describe how the judicial stare becomes a precondition for the texts' guarantees of objectivity which (somehow) present themselves as being both before and beyond the 'reality' which they attempt to appropriate in discourse.

First, then, we will describe how adjudicative narrative, engendering an official hierarchy of knowing subjects, was employed to inquire 'into the circumstances in which it was possible for Detective Sergeant Harold Gordon Challenor of the Metropolitan Police to continue on duty at a time when he appears to have been affected by the onset of mental illness' (HMSO, 1965).

Adjudicative narrative and the hierarchy of knowing subjects

As we have already argued, official inquiries into law and order problems are always, at root, attempted resolutions of legitimacy crises of various degrees of magnitude (e.g. quite minor in the case of Challenor's attempt to 'pervert the course of justice' and considerably greater in the events engendering Scarman's report on Northern Ireland (HMSO, 1972) and Grunwick (HMSO, 1977). The discursive task of a report of an official inquiry is at least

69

twofold: simultaneously it has to establish an implicit perspective whence authoritative judgment can be made regarding first, what actually happened *at the time*, and second, what those events really mean *for all time*. What is at stake in the James Report on Challenor is the maintainence of two opposing contentions: (i) *that it is established on the evidence of contemporary witnesses* that Sergeant Challenor was mentally ill at the time of planting pieces of brick on three suspects; and (ii) that the same witnesses whose evidence *now* establishes that Challenor was mentally ill could not have known that he was ill *at the time*. The resolution of the dilemma, posed by the ironical status of these representations of factual history which can, *now*, but not, *then*, constitute evidence of mental illness, is a triumph of adjudicative narrative. Such triumphant resolution is overdetermined by: syntagmatic and didactic textual arrangements concerning *what* can be asked and be known *when*, and by *whom*, about the narrative history in question; paradigmatic and didactic management of a narrative history, the meaning of which should be apparent to all judicious readers. This achievement is similar in form and substance to the common-law mode whereby judges are able to invoke the precedent of common-sense effect (pragmatism in its anterior mode) to overturn precedent, whilst at the same time maintainting the *principle* of precedent intact. This achievement is also the hallmark of empiricism, whether in its cynical (Humean) or complacent (Popperean) modes.

Judicial discourse in its pristine form is concerned with providing the jurisprudential justifications for the coercive and administrative practices of the State. What is striking about judicial discourse, when it is employed by judges and other legal personnel during public inquiries, is the versatility of the discursive methodology whereby it can be demonstrated that all aspects of life are amenable to judicial interpretation and closure. In so far as public inquiries are usually arbitrating between conflicting accounts and interpretations of events, the officially-approved version has to confront, incorporate and suppress the alternative, unofficial version. We call this alternative, unofficial version the Other of the discourse, and the Unspeakable. The sequential organisation and dispersion of concurrent series of events within the pages of the James Report are directed at the gradual dissipation and final negation of this Other.

In June 1964, at the Central Criminal Court, three police-officers were found guilty of conspiracy to pervert the course of justice. 'Detective Sergeant Challenor had stood indicted together with those police-officers . . . and had by verdict of a jury been found unfit to plead the charge' (HMSO, 1965, Cmnd 2735). The trial judge had expressed 'disturbance' that Challenor had been on duty at all on 11 July 1963, the day of the 'bricks episode', and it is this worry that, although known to be 'mentally unbalanced', Challenor had been allowed to continue with police duties, that the James Report has to allay. (The James Report on the Challenor case is exactly five sides long. The remaining 170 pages of the book comprise appendices, the longest of which, Appendix A, is concerned with the events which culminated in the conviction of the three police-officers and Challenor's certification of mental illness. When, therefore, we refer to 'the Report' we will be referring to the five pages which give an initial statement of the Inquiry's main findings and to the 150 pages of Appendix A.)

The usual organisation of official reports allows them to frame subsequently presented evidence within the interpretive parameters of the final findings. These are presented at the beginning of the book. The James Report is no exception. Briefly: James found that Challenor *was* suffering from paranoid schizophrenia whilst on duty, but that the nature of that illness is such that nobody could have been expected to recognise it as such at the time. The Other is also briefly confronted:

> It was submitted to me . . . that at West End Central Station . . .
> an atmosphere had developed whereby police-officers, and
> Detective Sergeant Challenor in particular, could use violence
> and show disrespect to persons in custody, and could indulge in
> fabrication of evidence without exciting attention. If the
> evidence established that such was the atmosphere at West End
> Central Police station it surely would have been a contributory
> cause to Detective Sergeant Challenor remaining on duty, and a
> serious situation . . . (HMSO, 1965, Cmnd 2735: 8).

And, in the next sentence, this Other is immediately rendered Unspeakable: 'I have reached the conclusion that the evidence does not support the submission made, and that there was no such cause enabling Detective Sergeant Challenor's mental illness to be undetected' (ibid.). Thereafter the James Report is organised in such a way that its readers also can be invited to interpret events from the site of epistemological privilege accorded to Mr A. E. James QC. First, (Part One, Chapter One) there is the lesson on the nature of paranoid schizophrenia. This chapter exemplifies common-law's

71

and common-sense's evolutionary slogan, '*Then* they didn't see it, *now* they do'! Common-sense (the layman's) and human nature are invoked to show how it is that what is *now* apparent to Mr James QC could not have been apparent (although existent) *then*, even to specialists in psychological medicine!

> At such a stage diagnosis of the illness, even by a specialist in psychological medicine, is exceedingly difficult, and, human nature being what it is, the layman would not think of attributing the symptoms to mental illness, but would readily find some physical explanation, such as overwork (Cmnd 2735: 11).

Chapter Two sees the entrance of our Hero. Challenor's biographical history to April 1963 is reconstructed and it is a highly punctuated selection of exemplary biographical items. Detailed description (including examination marks) of Challenor's army and police career is given, particular emphasis being laid on his appetite for hard work and his increasing worries about impending deafness. Having already had access to Mr James's privileged findings we 'see' the significance of the juxtaposition of these topics of chapters one and two. It is this exemplary police-sergeant of Chapter Two who is about to be struck down by that 'insidious' and nebulous disease, described in Chapter One and which *we* know is often perceived by witnesses as a sign of overwork, but whose manifestation is usually occasioned by the patient's being under some particular strain or worry. So to Chapter Three: Our Hero's stage. This too is exemplary. The techniques and assumptions of detailed positivistic description are employed to enjoin readers, via a subjectivist empiricism, to engage in a fraternal critique which 'sees' any mistaken practices occurring amongst the CID at West End Central Police Station as resulting from the obvious effects of overwork. Armed thus with our discursive knowledge of the Villain (paranoid schizophrenia), the Hero (our exemplary police-sergeant) and the Heroic Stage (West End Central Police Station), we are now allowed to view the evidence as it was presented by those less knowing than Mr James and his readers, those involved in frequent but (until now) discursively non-appropriated encounters with Detective Sergeant Challenor. And it is now, despite the syntagmatical arrangement of the normatively managed paradigms established in the first three chapters, that the Other frequently reappears, necessitating further techniques of dispersion, punctuation and closure to be employed.

During the twelve-month period from September 1962 to September 1963 there were eight separate incidents resulting in public complaint against Detective Sergeant Challenor. With one exception, these incidents were concentrated in the period April–6 September 1963. From May 1963, there is evidence that Challenor's superiors at West End Central Police Station were increasingly viewing his activities as an embarrassment. Approaches to management (up to Deputy Commander level) were made to get Challenor removed to another station. Attempts were made to keep him off the streets of the West End. Twice Challenor was obliged to see the Consultant Physician to the Metropolitan Police: repeatedly he was passed as being fit for duty. From mid-August to mid-October 1963 Challenor was shuttled back and forth between his station-officers (who didn't know what to do with him) and a whole battery of doctors, including psychologists and psychiatrists, who were reluctant to diagnose mental illness. But the effective decisions were not to be made by psychiatrists or psychologists. After Challenor's NHS doctor had passed him fit for duty on 21 September, 1963, and after the Consultant Psychiatrist at St Thomas's Hospital had examined him on 15 October, and reported: 'I do not see how I can keep him off sick any longer,' Challenor's superior officer at West End Central simply refused to accept this and Challenor was returned to yet another psychologist. The new psychologist, Dr Sargent, was forewarned. The Consultant Physician to the Metropolitan Police wrote to him: 'I feel that he [Challenor] is totally abnormal but Barlow's recent report makes it extremely difficult to act in this man's interest, namely, to keep him off duty until he becomes his normal self again.' On 25 October Dr Sargent reported his findings . . . 'I am certain that Harold Challenor is very mad indeed . . . I am sure he is covering a mass of delusional ideas . . . I consider him certifiably insane. . . .' (HMSO, 1965, Cmnd 2735.41). Which is what the privileged readers of the James Report knew already. What the Report has to do therefore is to establish the rectitude of its narrative logic, a logic whose lacunae effectively establish that what happened at West End Central Police Station cannot adequately be appropriated by that narrative (which is why official reports seldom make sense to readers who attempt to read them via the texts' own declared logics.) Frankfurter has made the same point about the reading of statutes: 'The process of construction, therefore, is not an exercise in logic or dialectic: the aids of formal reasoning are not irrelevant; they may simply be inadequate'

(Frankfurter, 1964: 45). In the James Report the rectitude of narrative logic is established by three interrelated techniques:

The privileging as knowing subjects of author, readers and characters within the narrative

Throughout the James Report the privileged position of the Author
is asserted as the major guarantee of the correctness of the findings.
Where James's findings might appear to contradict either the interpretations of contemporary witnesses or the fragile narrative logic
realised by the remainder of the discursive text, one of three
varieties of empiricism is invoked. The first form of empiricism we
call *moral positivist* empiricism. Moral positivism establishes the
credibility (or not) of the characters in the text. With the introduction of each new character the reader is invited to trust the
privileged judgment of those who, because they actually saw and
heard the witnesses are best empowered to judge the credibility of
their representations of events. This moral positivist empiricism
allows Mr James to privilege Mrs Challenor as 'a most impressive
and frank witness' (p. 35) and Mr Rooum, one unfortunate bene-
ficiary of Challenor's brick-planting antics, as someone who 'was
well versed in his evidence, and [whose] apparent enjoyment in the
giving thereof detracted from its objectivity and the weight which
could be given to it' (ibid., p. 102). For Mr James knows an anarchist when he sees one! Having stated that Mr Rooum described
himself as 'an Anarchist and a member of the National Council of
Civil Liberties', Mr James remarks rather esoterically that, 'his
evidence and demeanour at the inquiry confirmed this' (ibid.).

The second empiricist mode is that of *subjectivist* empiricism.
Here neither the Author nor his readers witnessed the actual events
in question, but because of an intersubjectivity rooted in the human
conditions judicious official discourse can guarantee its assertions of
fact by claiming that anyone would understand why the characters
(they are not fate-bearing actors in the Greek dramatic tradition,
they are moral characters in the Christian dramatic tradition) acted
as indeed the discursive text has asserted that they did act. (Indeed,
in recognition of the qualities necessary to subjectivist empiricist
interpretation, Mr James thanks at the outset the Inquiry's Assessor
for his 'experience and understanding of human-nature [upon
which] I have made heavy calls' (ibid., p. 9).)

The third empiricist mode is that of *evolutionary* empiricism. This mode claims that those who have access to the greatest number of descriptive items of an event are both those with the most complete picture of what happened *and* those best situated to adjudicate between contradictory descriptions. Although, on its own, this is the crudest form of empiricism, its paradigmatic (metaphoric) and syntagmatic (metonymic) insemination of narrative time and narrative relevance renders it the lynchpin of narrative logic.

The privileging of narrative time

The central theme of this paper has been the description and redescription of the techniques common to common-law, common-sense and epistemology. We have been arguing that these techniques reproduce the tautologous (and continuously disappearing) guarantees of their own real logics (legitimacy). An important element in this reproductive scheme is the rigid control and management of narrative time.

The temporal logic of the James Report was determined extradiscursively. It was partly determined by the posing of the Official question which engendered the report: how was it that Challenor could continue on duty at a time when he appears to have been mentally ill? It was partly determined by the Unofficial answer which is confronted at the beginning of the Report: Challenor could continue on duty whilst he was manifesting symptoms of mental illness because his violent and lawless behaviour was seen as normal at West End Central, where it did not markedly deviate from the behaviour of many other police-officers. The object (desire-Lacan, 1966) of the discourse is to assert that Challenor's behaviour whilst he was on duty was in fact *so* deviant from normal police practice at West End Central that it *did* constitute the behaviours which are symptomatic of paranoid schizophrenia, but that at the same time the essential nature of that illness rendered it invisible to Challenor's colleagues. The job (desire-Freud, 1976) of the discourse is to enable the reader to recognise the discursive object for what it really is: authoritative absolution from blame of lawenforcers whose image of rectitude has been tarnished by the Challenor case. This is similar to the desire of common-law jurisprudence and of epistemology. When each is concerned with claiming that real events can be discursively appropriated, moral and knowing subjects have to be temporally and spatially located in the ideal place whence their situated actions, their motives and interpretations can be shown to be at one with the logic of the text.

The positivistic description occasioned by the empiricist method of the James Report informs its readers that during the period 25 April to 11 July 1963, there occurred, at West End Central Police Station, seven incidents which subsequently resulted in complaints against Detective Sergeant Challenor. A phenomenology of these events would describe a situation where a detective sergeant was increasingly becoming an embarrassment to his superiors who, though beset on all sides by complaints against him, were apparently unable to curb his acknowledged departures from legitimate police procedures. But the readers of the James Report are not presented with a phenomenology. (They have to constitute this themselves via an unofficial reading of the text). Instead they are presented with an episodic history. The three months up to and including 11 July (the day of the 'brick' incident) are fragmented and presented as a series of separate moments ('episodes') in the history of West End Central Police Station. Seven temporally distinct episodes (an eighth involves an incident in September 1962) are presented in seven separate chapters. At the end of each chapter James can 'reasonably' conclude that in relation to the incidents described in that chapter, and within the discursive parameters of that particular episode, it would be unreasonable to expect anyone to have hazarded an opinion that Challenor was mentally ill. That *de facto* some people *did* hazard such a guess can be appropriated by the didactic techniques, which instruct the reader on how to appropriate the seemingly contradictory meanings of the empirical descriptions. For judicial discourse, like common-sense and epistemology, always constructs a place whence it can go beyond the posited guarantees of its own object.

The privileging of narrative logic

There are many ways to tell the same story, to make very different points, or to make no point at all. Pointless stories are met (in English) with the withering rejoinder, 'So what?' Every good narrator is continually warding off this question (Labov, 1972, quoted in Pratt, 1977).

We have argued previously that Official Discourse is didactic. Any discourse is didactic in so far as it provides sets of directions as to how it can (legitimately) be read. But Official Discourse sets up its own credentials in such a way that it can both hammer home the point of its own story *and* adjudicate between the other versions of the story, incorporating some versions, over-ruling others.

In the James Report, moral, subjectivist and evolutionary empiricisms distribute epistemological rights, duties and obligations to different characters (and to the reader) according to the points at which they are allowed to step into the narrative history. Thus, according to the logic of our narrative it is understandable that some people at the time *did* think that Challenor was mentally ill: they can be absolved from the blame of being right for the wrong reasons because it can be shown that they had no access to the situational logic of other, more privileged characters. Consider, finally, the case of the superintendent from Tottenham Court Road Police Station who *did* diagnose Challenor as being mentally ill:

> That which was novel and startling to Superintendent Burdett fitted readily into Detective Superintendent Townsend's already formed opinion that Detective Sergeant Challenor was a very tired, overworked officer suffering from the strain of increasing deafness (ibid., p. 23).

Which statement neatly summarises one claim which is implicit in common-law, common-sense and empiricist reasoning: that those in command of the most facts are best situated to adjudicate between them, even though, (as the facts always are supposed to exist beyond the discourse in which it is supposed that they can be known) these privileged adjudicators may subsequently be found to be wrong. Until then . . . there are technical guarantees to render inviolate those places of epistemological and judicial privilege whence the privileged can speak.

Technical guarantees of objectivity and the discursive appropriation of a material world

We have argued that judicial discourse necessitates the creation of a space from which the judicial agent, as the mediated embodiment of justice, speaks. This knowing subject is ostensibly placed within the discursive constraints of the normative rationalism and precedential empiricism of the common law mode. Common-sense is invoked to instruct the ideal addressee of the discourse that judicial mediation is neither arbitrary nor pragmatic but the determinative product of discursive juridicial relations:

Diplock on Grunwick:

> Lord Diplock said that the appeal was concerned with one facet
> of an industrial dispute which had engendered a good deal of
> political heat and unfortunately still continued to do. That facet
> did not involve their Lordships forming, let alone expressing,
> any views as to the merits or conduct of either Grunwick or
> Apex. All that fell to be decided was a naked question of law, the
> true construction of sections 11 to 16 of the Employment
> Protection Act, 1975 . . . and in particular on the meaning of
> section 14 (1) (*Times* Law Report 15 December 1977).

It is this type of intra-discursive logic that constitutes the technical
guarantees of judicial objectivity. The knowing subject is constrained by the logic of the facts of historical continuity fashioned by
the essential principles of justice. These technical guarantees take
the form of applying the law that is within the procedural rules of
due process. What follows in this section is an analysis of a systematic attack on some of these guarantees that are contained in the
Diplock Report of the Commission to 'consider legal procedures to
deal with terrorist activities in Northern Ireland' (Diplock, 1972).
We shall be interested to demonstrate how these controls on the
knowing subject are jettisoned in the name of an idealised essential
justice via, however, a mode of argument that remains within
common-law discourse. The controls on the subject-who-is-
supposed-to-know turn out to be pragmatic licence.

The Diplock Report was commissioned to consider what changes
could be made in order to reduce the number of 'terrorists' being
interned or detained and to increase the number of 'terrorists'
standing trial in a court of law. The report acknowledges that
detention tribunals cannot be seen to be fair (para. 33) and should
not therefore 'be regarded or described as an ordinary court of law
or as forming part of the regular judicial system or should be
composed of judges who also sit in the regular courts in Northern
Ireland' (ibid.: para. 12). The report would like to be in a position to
dispense with detention tribunals and to replace them with trials
that comply with the minimum requirements of Article 6 of the
European Convention for the Protection of Human Rights and
Fundamental Freedoms (that international humanist Other which
is increasingly punctuating common law discourse). However, even
though it is willing to recommend changes in legal practice to effect

this transition, such as trials *in camera*, and alterations in the rules of evidence (so that, for example, the onus of proof of non-member-ship of a terrorist organisation lay with the defendant; attendance at an illegal meeting would be proof of membership . . .), the major problems would still remain. The objections to implementing such changes are entirely practical – they simply will not work. Trials *in camera* with witnesses behind screens, with the accused absent, will still not remove the fear of the intimidation of witnesses as the defence lawyer would have to be present and witnesses would not believe that their identity would remain safe from the defendant. Similarly changing rules on the onus of proof of membership of an illegal organisation is in 'principle' (para. 25) unproblematic but 'in practice we doubt whether under the conditions now existing in Northern Ireland this would have much effect' (ibid.).

The Commissioners are thus caught in a double bind: detention does not comply with the technical guarantees of objectivity and changes within these guarantees, in compliance with the Other of international legalism, are not able to appropriate the material reality of terrorist resistance:

> The dilemma is complete. The only hope of restoring the efficacy of criminal courts of law in Northern Ireland is by using an extra-judicial process to deprive of their ability to operate in Northern Ireland, those terrorists whose activities result in the intimidation of witnesses (para. 27).

At this juncture of the text the discursive logic is in complete disarray: the conditions of existence of courts of law are detention tribunals for difficult cases. Wilden (1972: 223) writes of the paradox: 'The axioms generate statements of a logical type different from all other statements in the system, and all attempts to deal with those sentences without transcending the epistemology which pro-duced them result in irresolvable paradoxes'. It is precisely at such a point of paradox that the pragmatist circle of common-law reason-ing is invoked in an attempt to repair the legitimation deficit.

In the next, remarkable, passage we learn that technical guarantees can inhibit the realisation of justice, common sense tells us this, and that their suspension can, therefore, re-locate the administration of justice once again within the proper tradition of the common law. Detention, we are informed, does not mean:

> imprisonment at the arbitrary Diktat of the Executive

Government . . . We use it to describe depriving a man of his liberty as a result of an investigation of the facts which inculpate the detainee by an impartial person or tribunal by making use of a procedure which, however fair to him, is inappropriate to a court of law because it does not comply with Article 6 of the European Convention. Lawyers, particularly English and Irish lawyers, tend to assume that the only safe evidence on which to commit a man upon a criminal charge is that which is admitted and elicited in accordance with the technical rules of procedure which are at present used in English and Northern Irish criminal courts and are stricter in favour of the accused than those followed in the Courts of other countries in Europe. But in fact there may be material available to the security authorities which would carry complete conviction as to the guilt of the accused to any impartial arbiter of common sense, although it is based on statements by witnesses who cannot be subject to questioning by lawyers on behalf of the accused or even produced for examination by the arbiter himself. If there is any process by which members of terrorist organisations can be identified with certainty their detention in custody does not involve the punishment of an innocent man, or even one who is guilty of what could be properly called only a 'political crime'. It means depriving of his liberty albeit by an extra-judicial process, a criminal who has committed an offence which has been punishable by the common law of England and Northern Ireland for upwards of two centuries before the current emergency arose (paras 28–9).

Here we are assured that the detention machinery has its own guarantees which though different from the normal procedures are ensured by the dictates of common sense to replace the administration of justice into the well-worn grooves of the historical continuity of common-law principles. Those technical guarantees are later elaborated as the cross checking of informants' evidence (which must learn from the mistakes of internment) and their presentation to the 'fresh minds' of the 'impartial arbiter' (para. 31.2).

If the first discursive shift to extricate the text from its double-bind is a re-location of detention as *essentially* though not *evidentially* just, the second move is to re-structure the technical guarantees of the courts themselves, so that more cases can be heard there rather than in the tribunals. The text now moves, and at a pace that would leave the most pragmatic breathless, to dismantle whole sections of the procedure of due process for certain scheduled offences: juries are abolished, the laws of arrest fundamentally altered, conditions for bail drastically curtailed, the onus of proof of possession reversed, and the admissibility of statements of confession and evidence of witnesses radically changed. How can this almost new legal system, implemented and functioning at present as the Diplock courts in the North of Ireland, be justified?

First the normative rationalist essence of legal principles is invoked over the technicalities of precedent, while second, and simultaneously, the legal changes are re-established within the unfolding verisimilitude of the historico-legal tradition. The logic of this discursive appropriation is *plus ça change, plus c'est la même chose*, the effectivity an instrumental adjustment to material change.

Let us unfold the manner in which the laws of arrest are changed. 'In normal times' an arrest is made by a police officer who informs the person arrested of the reason for his arrest. In Northern Ireland 'it is not practicable' that this be applied to the potential terrorist, indeed the commissioners think it 'preposterous to expect a young soldier' to inform a suspected terrorist of the reason for his arrest: 'Yet the courts in Northern Ireland apply the ordinary common law rules as making it necessary for the soldiers who first apprehend the suspect to inform him accurately of the ground on which he is being arrested' (para. 46). Accordingly they propose recommendations allowing an arrest to a police station or barracks of a person suspected of any terrorist offence, to hold the suspect for four hours and to make it an offence if the suspect does not co-operate. This abdication of technical guarantees is necessary as:

> Reluctant though we are to propose any curtailment, however slight, of the liberty of any innocent man we think it is justified to take the risk that occasionally a person who takes no part in terrorist activity and has no special knowledge about terrorist organisation shall be detained for such short time as is needed to establish his identity, rather than that dangerous and guilty men should escape justice because of technical rules about arrest to which it is impracticable to conform in existing conditions (para. 48).

After this demonstration that present conditions no longer mesh with common-law rules we are witness to an evolutionary mutation:

81

legal selection breaks through the technical constraints of a past environment to let justice adapt to the current ecology. Just in case the critical reader might fear the legal mutant to be a dangerous hybrid we are immediately returned to common-law rhetoric:

> Nothing that we propose to simplify the formalities of arrest by members of the armed forces should be understood as countenancing any relaxation of their common law obligation to use no more than that amount of force that is reasonably necessary in all circumstances to effect the arrest and hold the arrested person in custody (para. 50).

Having established this discursive terrorism as a normal mode of appropriation the text moves into an offensive assault. We are instructed of the 'highly technical rules of English law' upon the admissibility of confessions originating 'at a period when the accused was prohibited from giving evidence at his own trial' (para. 73). But now 'as the law has developed since this handicap on the accused has been removed, the test of admissibility has become subject to a number of technical rules' (para. 79) embodied in past decisions and the Judges Rules. These rules 'are hampering the course of justice in the case of terrorist crimes' and are changed by the commissioners so that the 'urge to confide' in one's interrogator which produces inculpatory admissions can be reproduced in court:

> We do not think that with human life and property so gravely at risk any fair-minded man would consider that in the present emergency the police who are charged with the detection of crime should be discouraged from creating by means which do not involve physical violence or the threat of it or any other human or degrading treatment, a situation in which a guilty man is more likely than he would be otherwise to overcome his initial reluctance to speak and to unburden himself to his questioners (para. 91).

Similarly, and finally, the pragmatist instrumentalism of the common law mode is evidenced in the juggling of principles and rules on the onus of proof of possession:

> There are two technical rules of English and Northern Irish Criminal law and procedure which greatly enhance the difficulty of obtaining convictions of guilty men in the exceptional

circumstances which now exist in Northern Ireland. They relate to the onus of proof of possession and to the admissibility of confessions. We call them 'technical rules' because they are peculiar to English law and legal systems which derive from it. No similar rules are to be found in legal systems based on the civil law which are in force in other European countries nor are they called for to satisfy the requirements of the European Convention. But they are also technical in a much more fundamental sense: they are not essential for the protection of the innocent . . . as they are applied by the Courts in Northern Ireland they result in the acquittal of significant numbers of those who are undoubtedly guilty of terrorist crimes.

It follows then that the amendment of outmoded technicist con- straints would lead the courts closer to juridical verisimilitude, the relaxation of these technicalities would have meant that: 'a convic- tion could have been obtained as a result of a fair trial in open court in accordance with a procedure which in the emergency which now exists in Northern Ireland any fair-minded man in England or elsewhere in Europe would regard as just and as appropriate to a court of law' (para. 60). With respect to possession of arms, ammunition and explosives these judicial authorities recommend a change in the law so that the onus of proof falls upon the defendant, yet once again we are left in a common law groove: 'This would leave untouched the common law defence that the accused was acting under duress: that he was compelled to store the lethal objects against his will by imminent threats to his safety or that of his wife or family' (para. 72).

The Diplock text's radical transformation of due process leans heavily upon the invocation of the abnormal conditions in Northern Ireland which render the technical guarantees of judicial objectivity 'impracticable'. These abnormalities bestow upon the text a discur- sive confidence that clearly exposes the pragmatist nature of juridical precedent. Far from judicial subjects being held within the conceptual net of precedent and principle we see how easily the space occupied by the state and its judicial mediators is one of pragmatic instrumentality. Its intra-discursive logic is as incoherent as its epistemological justification. Though argued in terms of essentialised justice, re-located within legal evolution, the changes in the technical guarantees of objectivity remain but a part of the syntagmatic strategy which orders the paradigms of the common law mode towards a unity of its discursive object: the discursive appropriation of an official world whose Otherness is beyond Recognition.

The object of judicial discourse, the intentional goal of the communication between its idealist sender and its ideal addressee, is precisely the appropriation of a legitimation deficit engendered by the material reality of actual social relations. Wilden (1972: 35) writes that:

> In language there is a very large number of ways of saying the same thing, and in an infinite number of possible messages. Determined as it is by its code and by its syntax, language is perhaps the most semiotically free of all representational and communicational systems – and it is not ruled by causality, but by possibility, constraint, and by its pragmatic-semantic function, that of the transmission and reproduction of variety in the system.

In *discourse* it is the object of appropriation, the Other, which delineates the selectivity of these paradigms and the combinations of the syntactical form. In judicial discourse the Other is ultimately the relations of class contradiction that become the object of an attempt to be pushed through the sieve of an idealised essential justice. The desire to appropriate the real through the ideal produces a discourse locked into the imaginary, that is ordered by a fantastic conception of justice. The result is that: 'The manifest discourse, therefore, is really no more than the repressive presence of what it does not say; and this "not-said" is a hollow that undermines from within all that is said' (Foucault, 1972: 25).

To this extent judicial discourse is an attempt to exclude the discourse of the Other from the sense of the texts. For example, in Diplock we have shown that the detention tribunals are simultaneously argued as indispensable (para. 27) and as also residing outside 'the regular judicial system' (paras. 12, 27). The text becomes an attempt to maintain the credibility of the regular judicial system. The systematic attempt (Chapters 5 to 10) to place the recommended changes to the regular system within Article 6 of the European Convention is rendered absurd by the reality that 'terrorism' and the tribunal system itself stand as the fifth columnists undermining from within this quest for legitimacy:

The judiciary has nevertheless managed to retain a reputation for impartiality which arises above the divisive conflict which has effected so many other functions of government in the province; and the courts of law and the procedures that they use have in general held the respect and trust of all except the extremists of both factions. We regard it as of paramount importance that the criminal courts of law and judges and resident magistrates who preside in them should continue to retain that respect and trust throughout the emergency and after the emergency has come to an end. If anything were done which weakened it, it might take generations to rebuild, for in Northern Ireland memories are very long. For this reason we would find ourselves unable to recommend any changes in the conduct of a criminal trial of terrorist offences in a court of law in Northern Ireland which would have the result that it no longer complied with the minimum requirements of Article 6 of the European Convention (paras 13–14).

The subsequent discourse on the technical guarantees of objectivity within the common law mode is subject to the reader colluding in the notion that detention is an entirely separate matter from the regular judicial system. This no man's land is precisely where the Other resides and cannot be expunged by the exhalted claims of judicial fiat.

If Diplock on Northern Ireland is instructive because of its two-tiered approach to material appropriation, Scarman (HMSO, 1977) on Grunwick is illustrative of a position when the law finds itself with *no* place to appropriate from. In this 'Report of an inquiry under the Rt Hon. Lord Justice Scarman, OBE, into a dispute between Grunwick Processing Laboratories and members of the Association of Professional, Executive, Clerical and Computer Staff' the Other appears in the form of a Recognition that the laws of the production and reproduction of value are of a different order to the law itself:

In our judgement, good industrial relations depend upon a willingness to co-operate and compromise. The law favours collective bargaining and encourages the use by workers of independent trade unions for the purpose. The policy of the law is to exclude 'trade disputes' from judicial review by the courts and to rely not on the compulsory processes of the law but on the voluntary approach, backed by advice, conciliation, and arbitration to promote good industrial relations (para. 72).

85

So it is that the most salient form of the Other of industrial conflict is excluded from 'the compulsory processes of the law'. The acknowledgment of this absence leaves the discursive regularities of judicial discourse redundant. We still witness the attempt to appropriate this object into legal discourse:

> In the field of industrial relations the law has to effect a reconciliation and adjustment of a number of fundamental rights and freedoms . . . (these are then stipulated in terms of Articles of the Universal Declaration and European Convention) . . . The English reconciliation of these rights and freedoms has been traditionally sought through the development of voluntary collective bargaining but this process is now supported principally by two statutes, which themselves have to be interpreted in the context of the common law – the backcloth of English Law (paras 55.8).

Yet these two statutes (the Trade Union and Labour Relations Act 1974 and the Employment Protection Act 1975) have been designed to exclude trade disputes from judicial review. The judicial magician has lost his wand. The recourse is to extend the 'spirit of the law' into the norms of industrial relations:

> English law, if it is to work, requires of parties to an industrial dispute a modicum of self-restraint in the pursuit of their rights. Men must act reasonably *within* the law. The British tradition of compromise is implicit in the modern English law governing industrial relations. Judged by the norms of good industrial relations practice that are to be found in industry generally, how have the company and the union measured up to the *responsibilities imposed upon them by law but not directly enforceable by legal process*? (emphasis added) (para. 58.9).

The application of these extra-judicial criteria results in the finding: 'On the legal aspect of the dispute we conclude that both the company and the union have in certain respects failed to respond to the spirit of the law' (para. 64).

For whatever historical reasons the law has left many aspects of industrial disputes unregulated. Therefore when such a dispute as the Grunwick struggle becomes a national issue the attempt to appropriate the problem through a court of inquiry flounders in the space of judicial irrelevance to produce limp appeals to the norms of industrial relations and the spirit of the policy of the law. The subtleties of judicial discourse become inoperable when it recognises an Other that resides outside the boundaries of its sphere of appropriation. The technical guarantees of objectivity cannot even be invoked: the outcome of struggle is not effected by common-sense, common-law or epistemology.

6 Official Discourse

Narcissus was forever grasping his shadow. What was the object of his own desire but what eluded him was himself: the mirror did not give him himself, because the only one in the world he had to tell him what he was, was Echo, the absolute Other, to whom none could get attached because she would not listen and who did no more than repeat the words of Narcissus' own self-fascination (Juliet Mitchell, 1974: 39).

The judicial stare is one particularly effective discursive formation epistemically available to an Official Discourse. Within the *archival* formation of an Official Discourse however judicial modalities must be further transformed. It is the Lawgiver who must speak but it is the Statesman who must listen. Official Discourse cannot only listen to and speak to the Judge. The authority of the Lawgiver has to inseminate the already-known history of a capitalist state claiming legitimacy under the political sign of democracy. The authority of the Lawgiver has to be unveiled at an 'intersubjective' place where natural reason resides. It is in this place that the bond between Lawgiver and knowing subject is to be cemented.

This chapter analyses two more official reports on law and order issues: the Devlin Report on identification parades and the Scarman Report on the 1969 disturbances in Northern Ireland. The Devlin Report was engendered by the wrongful imprisonment of two men, Laszlo Virag and Luke Dougherty. The Scarman Report was engendered by complaints about police behaviour during the 1969 disturbances. We have characterised the discursive practices realised by these reports as being both pedagogic and repressive. In this chapter we attempt not only to locate and reassemble the metonymised discourses which are embedded in the texts but also to argue that the total discursive formation is ordered by the desire both to confront and suppress the dominant signifiers of an Other – the social relations of a capitalist state.

Discursive problems of official publications on law and order

Habermas (1976) has suggested that the state represents mono-polistic discourse. Yet, on the contrary, Official Discourse maintains that the legitimacy of state practice can be justified against critique. State discourse does indeed tacitly accept and propagate the 'ideal speech situation' in which validity claims over justice can be discursively redeemed. But Habermas's definition is ideal-typical and not ironical. He writes:

> Discourse can be understood as that form of communication that is removed from contexts of experience and action and whose structure assures us: that the bracketed validity claims of assertions, recommendations or warnings are the exclusive object of that discussion; that participants, themes and contributions are not restricted except with reference to the goal of testing the validity claims in question; that no force except that of the better argument is exercised and that as a result all motives except that of the co-operation search for truth are excluded (1976: 106).

The following analysis of Official Discourse argues that the state exploits this ideal-typical definition of discourse in the service of repressive practices far removed from 'a co-operative search for truth'. The problems engendered by such apparently contradictory practice are resolved by an Official Discourse which continuously redefines the knowing subjects and known objects of the state and its apparatuses.

In reading these two reports we addressed once more the questions of authorship and readership. We asked:

1 To what silent accusations, and in whose name, do the Official reports reply?

2 How does the metonymic transference of elements from the pure signifiers produce the discursive power (plausibility) of the text?

Desirability of the Discourse

Official Discourse, in the two publications we studied, addressed itself to the desirability and possibility of its own legitimacy. Reconstitution and recognition of the knowing inter-subjectivity of legitimated state activities was the first priority, formulation of the possibilities for future authoritative address was the second. Lacan again (1975: 63):

> I identify myself in language, but only in losing myself in it like an object. What is realised in my history is not the past definite of what was, since it is no more, or even the present perfect of what has been in what I am, but the future anterior of what I shall have been for what I am in the process of becoming.

The authors of our publications identified themselves initially as empiricist interpreters of the capitalist state. The discourse of the Devlin Report, we were told, was made possible by the evidence of fifty-eight witnesses (individuals or institutions) evidence from six other countries and by study of at least seventeen publications, as well as all 'notable cases which have occurred over the last 100 years' (HC 338.189). But although the state was ostensibly engaging in empiricist reflexivity the occasion for that reflexivity was generated by the correct functioning of the state itself. For on the very first page it is stated that, although Virag and Dougherty were victims of what the Report terms 'miscarriages of justice' these were themselves both constituted and negated as such by the normal, articulated practices of the state apparatuses:

> In Virag's case the miscarriage was eventually discovered by enquiries *initiated* by the *police* and in the *Home Office* as a result of evidence obtained when the true criminal was arrested for other offences. This new evidence was so compelling as to recommend *The Queen* to pardon and release Mr. Virag without a reference to the courts (HC 338:1.1. our emphases).

Where, then, is the problem? With the Police, the Home Office and the Queen herself mediating justice – why bother to plough through the tedious and repetitive 157 pages of the Devlin Report? Because we are no longer concerned with justice at all. The major part of the Report is concerned with repairing the socio-technology in which images of justice must be prefabricated. The overt parameters of the enquiry have already shifted when, in the Report's second paragraph, it is stated that:

> *Honest but mistaken* identification by prosecution witnesses was the prime cause of the miscarriages of justice in the Dougherty and Virag cases and thus leads to the third limb of our enquiry i.e. an examination of the *rules and practice* governing evidence of identification in criminal cases (HC 338:1, para 1.2).

We have also had constituted for us, in these two opening paragraphs, the ideal knowing subject of the Official Discourse; he who knows that justice is the Ideal of the state and that when justice appears not to be done then the state itself, in adjusting its rules and practices, is prime mover in remedying the appearances which will in future be invoked as authorisations of its reality. So it is difficult to see why a further 156 pages before the Report can conclude:

> We have kept statutory change to a minimum believing that what is chiefly needed is a *change of attitude* by all those who are concerned in the handling of cases of disputed identity. . . . This change is best brought about by judicial development of the law and practice. We have pointed to the directions which this might take. Those passages cannot be put into summary form, but we *venture to hope* that they may be useful to the judges (ibid.: 156).

We have the intervening 154 pages because there is an absence in the text, an absence which structures a discourse whose conclusion resurrects its own geneses.

Between paragraph 1.1 of the Report and paragraph 1.2 resides the absences of the legitimated evidence engendered by the remainder of the discursive text. This absence instantly defines the parameters of a discourse in which the state can talk to its own constituents. It is recognition of this absence which entails the empirical presentation of other candidates for discursive re-presentation. The text, therefore, is disarmingly punctuated by the presentation of others, subjects and objects of a discourse which is *not* ideal.

Readers of the Devlin Report who are overawed by the first paragraph's celebration of its own omniscient rectitude will be relieved to find that other characters, less knowing, and certainly more fallible, are materialised in the text. On page 2, for instance, we are introduced to (and dismiss!) the 'foreign jurist' who might be critical of the judicial system. On page 7 we have to recognise and deal with a more immediate threat 'the liberal-minded critic of the existing law'; and throughout the text there is the irritating presence of the two victims themselves. Stubbornly they stalk the pages of the text, rendered incomprehensible by their judicial incompetence and their inexplicable silences. At the time of their arrests they both had a criminal record; they were both unemployed and one was a refugee of foreign birth. They have to be re-absorbed into the discursive ideality of a judicial system whose presented material contours continually puncture the desired unity of that discourse. In turn, we painfully learn of a solicitor who does not thoroughly investigate the alibi of his working-class client, of a Legal Aid system which undoubtedly disadvantages working-class clients at the Appeal stage, and of the 'misjudgement' in the Home Office which delayed the release of Mr Virag for two years. Finally, in reading of a police practice commonly employed to identify a suspect, we learn where the criminal population comes from; on page 73 of the Report we read that: 'The witness, accompanied by the police, keeps watch on a public place, for example, a crowd leaving a factory gate, or a labour exchange' (ibid.: p. 73, para. 4.16).

Thus has the state, in empirically and disarmingly examining its own reflection, to recognise and repair its own contrived distortions before it can arbitrate between them. The Other has to be faced before it can be conquered. At some stage the absent Other has to be obliterated from the mirror of the discourse and incorporated into the discourse itself. The Other of Official Discourse can only be *presented* as a legitimation deficit and the contrived legitimation deficit which the Devlin Report has to repair is partially stated once and for all on page 5 of the Report: 'In criminal cases the state has in the police an agency for the discovery of evidence superior to anything which the wealthiest defendant could employ' (ibid.: p. 5, para. 1.17).

Here, in fragmented form, is a glimpse of the already atrophied Other of the discourse, the Other which makes the Official Discourse both desirable and impossible. This Other, which can be reconstituted, through a theoretical reading of the text, as the material source of the state's ideality, renders the discourse desirable because 'desire ultimately seeks the annihilation of the other as an independent subject' (Wilden, 1975); it renders the discourse impossible, because, as the discourse itself reveals, and as Habermas has reiterated 'In the final analysis, the class structure is the source of the legitimation deficit' (Habermas, 1976: 73).

It is precisely such a fundamental legitimation crisis which the Scarman Report confronts. The phrase 'legitimation deficit' is hardly appropriate here. The situation in Northern Ireland is also one of both a hegemonic and political crisis. Yet material events are still remedied by a normative grid whose parameters have already been materially destroyed by the 'troubles' which called it into service and into question.

The British state's reaction to the civil conflict in Northern Ireland was, initially, one of appeasement to the Catholic minority population. Under pressure from Westminster the Stormont regime instigated marginal reform programmes. After the August 1969 riots reform packages came direct from Westminster. Those policies of placation towards the Civil Rights movement represented in general terms, a state intervention on behalf of interests of international and monopoly capital, whose political aims were a bourgeois democratic Six Counties. This intervention was against the policies of the fraction of Ulster capital, in alliance with petty-bourgeois and proletarian Orangeism, whose aims were that of the *status quo ante*. Legitimation for this intervention was partially sought through a series of commissions of inquiry into the troubles. They reported on the causes of the strife and made recommendation for its amelioration. Thus the Cameron Report (Cameron, 1969) set up on 15 January 1969 was used by the Six County Prime Minister as a basis for reform; the Hunt Report (HMSO, 1969) was commissioned in August 1969 and its findings were used to abolish the Ulster Special Constabulary. In the same month, and under the same need to fill a growing void of legitimacy, the Scarman Tribunal started its investigations into a definite matter of 'urgent public importance' (HMSO, 1972b, 1) principally the Province's wide riots of that August.

It was against this background of a power struggle among Unionist politicians, the intervention of the Westminster government, the overt failure of the early reform programme, the aftermath of the largest riots in thirty-five years and the establishment of troops on to the streets of the Six Counties that the desirability of a judicial inquiry into the crisis of the Stormont government has to be situated.

The Tribunal's submission was very broad. It 'had leave' to inquire into most of the major incidents of political violence that had occurred in the Six Counties between March and 17 August 1969. This required detailed investigation into deaths, injuries and riots in Derry, Armagh, Dungiven, Dungannon, Coalisland, Newry and Belfast. The Tribunal had the power to summon witnesses to appear before it. The evidence they gave was considered inadmissable in any subsequent criminal trial and because the Tribunal was taking place in Northern Ireland witnesses were also informed that they would not be detained under the Special Powers Act in the light of the answers they gave to the Tribunal. Such an admission is in recognition of the materiality of the Other which the subsequent discourse seeks to destroy. The Tribunal sat for two years and five months, it cost £460,250 (approximately one fifth of the total cost of the riots), took evidence from 440 witnesses and produced a report running into two volumes.

By the time this report was published it was widely condemned within Northern Ireland as being largely irrelevant to a society that had since moved from community riots to guerrilla warfare. But this belated attempt to maintain the vestiges of legitimacy of the police in Northern Ireland is theoretically very relevant. Its text reveals the structure which Official Discourse takes by illuminating the modalities used to reconstitute the State's tarnished image of justice. The modalities in the text make up the regularities of the discursive formation. But although such regularities can be found within Official Discourse, its discursive formation is practical (i.e. directed at instrumental closure) rather than theoretical. The self-denying desirability of Official Discourse pre-empts the possibility of it being a theoretical discourse. As empiricist arbiter of the evidence of constituents whose material practices are rooted in material class relationships, state discourse has to recast those practices in the language of principle and human fallibility. In so doing it denies its conditions of existence. It is thus impossible for the state apparatuses to construct a discourse within which new knowledge of judicial practice can be forged. Instead, the evidence of the witnesses has to be punctuated, annihilated and finally resuscitated through the self-evident claims of the language of socio-technicist possibilities. These, by their very presentation, are forever and ideally locked in history.

Possibility of the Discourse

Although we are arguing that Official Discourse is directed at ideological closure, we are at the same time arguing that as a practical (or socio-technicist) discourse it has a material effectivity, i.e. it has an ideological effect. We are also arguing that the structure of Official Discourse is determined by its need to remedy what is presented as legitimation deficit, *full* recognition of which would undermine the possibilities for authoritative Official Discourse. This legitimation deficit has to be appropriated by, normatively accounted for, and, finally erased by, the discursive practices of the state. It would be a mistake to regard these practices as being totally repressive; they have a pedagogic dimension. Official Discourse instructs by example.

The main problem for Official Discourse on law and order is that all problems have to be discussed in terms of an ideal of distributive justice which cannot admit to the material conditions which render that ideal impossible. A discourse has to be developed which will both pre-empt and foreclose any theory within which questions could be posed which might destroy the pre-givens of that discourse. A paradigmatic and syntagmatic (Giglioli, 1972) structure has to be developed which will invite the reader to collude in the empiricist rationality of the text.

Paradigmaticity and syntagmaticity are interdependents. In explicating the paradigms of the Devlin Report and the syntax of the Scarman Report we argue that the effectivity of Official Discourse as a practical discourse is *partly* dependent upon its systematic selection and elevation of the normative explanations. These simultaneously ignore/or silence all material evidence that such explanation has already been rendered impotent and irrelevant by the material conditions which have contradicted and necessitated it.

The paradigms

In referring to paradigmaticity we refer to a speaker's selection from a range of possible alternatives (Giglioli, 1972). Chomsky calls such a selection a speaker's performance and the range of permissable alternates known to him his competence (Chomsky, 1965). Official Discourse in simultaneously recognising and repairing the legitimation deficit which makes the discourse desirable, has to manage the empirical description of both its material and ideal causes so that subsequently it can appear to choose judiciously between them. Thus, 'a system of dispersion' (Foucault, 1972: 37) becomes necessary and the discourse's coherence becomes dependent upon 'interplays of differences, distances, substitutions,

95

transformations'. Starting-points, discontinuities and endings reside in the discourse's silences about the genesis of its own desirability. (This was very apparent to Mungham and Bankowski when they commented on the findings of the James Report (HMSO, 1975) which investigated the distribution of the Criminal Business between the lower and higher courts (Mungham and Bankowski, 1977). Here we are trying to analyse the paradigmaticity of some of the discursive themes within the reports we studied.

The paradigm of adversary justice

At the root of the adversary system there are two great principles. The first is the protection of a suspect or accused against self-incrimination. The second is open justice (HC 338: 5. para. 1.17).

In Chapter One of the Devlin Report the authorities juxtapose the ideal and material depictions of adversary justice. Once the normative roots of justice have been established the material fruits can easily be presented as the misshapen offspring of their erring human progenitors. Point and counter-point demonstrate that ideal justice is impossible, but a muted legal positivism preserves and justifies the state's guardianship of the only law there is (cf. Duncanson, 1976). Appeals are made to the evolutionary character of the common law as being that of a natural product mediated by the essential rectitude of the judiciary and legal profession (cf. Cain, 1976). The following passage demonstrates how ideal conceptions of justice and real knowledge of existent social relations are juxtaposed in such a way that the law is preserved intact at the same time as provision is made for future legitimation deficits to be attributed to the non-judicial and unlawful actions of its human agents. Commenting on their own recognition that state and defendant are not equal adversaries in the posited quest for justice, the authorities explain:

So long as the matter is in the hands of the judges, they are likely to continue to act as occasion requires, solving each problem as it comes along. This is the way the common law was made. It has many advantages but it means that there are always uncertain areas of law and practice. In particular it means that in many situations the police do not know whether they are supposed to

96

be acting as adversaries of or as friends to the defendant and have nothing to guide them except the general notion that they should act fairly to everybody (HC 338: 5 para 1.19).

In this passage the paradigm is explicated: the sequence of authoritative appeal first sets up the evolutionary ideal, then it ironises it by depicting the material difficulties inhibiting its realisation. Finally a solution to the irony is suggested by invocation of the notion of natural justice (a notion incompletely realised now, but capable of complete realisation in the future). But the paradigm is incomplete. The Other of the discourse has not been recognised for purposes of legitimation but for the purpose of disarmament. The reader of chapter one of the Devlin Report, disarmed by the frequency (eight times in eight pages) with which the authorities have confronted the roots of their own legitimation deficit, scarcely notices that on page 7 of the text a common-sense conception of retributive state control is evoked as being the necessarily decisive principle of positive adversary justice.

> In the end and overall our recommendations are bound to mean that the benefit of a higher acquittal rate will be bestowed on the guilty as well as on the innocent. Some of the guilty will be violent criminals. In making our recommendations we have borne this constantly in mind and have endeavoured to strike a tolerable balance. Liberal-minded critics of the existing law and practice rarely, so far as we have seen, essay to count the cost of the reforms they suggest in terms of the criminals who will go free. In this country we are prepared to pay a very high figure in those terms, but it cannot be unlimited.

Ironically, of course, in evoking common-sense to destroy the Other, the authorities ideally define but materially destroy the imaginary parameters of their legitimacy.

The paradigm for explaining 'miscarriages of justice'

The paradigm for explaining 'miscarriages of justice' is basically the same as that for depicting the adversary justice system, though its syntagmatic arrangement activates its ideal connotations as it simultaneously suppresses its material constituencies. What is presented is a material description of an adversary justice system articulated by sets of class knowledges, whilst what pass as explanations are highly punctuated and atrophied descriptions of normative failure.

Consider the paradigm which the authorities invoke to explain the 'miscarriage of justice' and then look to the text itself to indicate the nature of the evidence which was *not* selected as having any explanatory value.

The exception rather than the rule　We have already described the state practices which we are investigating as having a pedagogic dimension. The first lesson which Official Discourse has to impress is that the material circumstances which engender threats to its legitimacy are exceptional rather than normal. The report of the inquiry into Dougherty's case recognised nine instances of either rule-breaking or failures to appreciate the already legitimated scope of a rule before claiming that 'a very unusual number of things went wrong in the case of *R. V. Dougherty*' (HC 338:28 para 2.63). Likewise, after being instructed that 'the main cause of the wrongful conviction and subsequent punishment of Mr. Virag was unquestionably the fact that he was wrongly identified' (HC 338:59 para 3.103) we are told, 54 pages later, that as far as the identification parade (the main posited object of inquiry) is concerned 'we are dealing with an institution which on the whole is working well. We have had some complaints but very few have been substantiated. The improvements suggested are mainly in matters of detail . . . amendments to or amplifications of, the existing rules. . . . We have heard little criticism of the good faith and impartiality with which they are administered'. Exactly 54 pages further on still (in an appendix) we are given an example of the relevance of that rule-governed impartiality when we learn how Virag was coerced into legitimating the identification parade where he was wrongly identified as the Liverpool criminal, and subsequently tried and sentenced to ten years' imprisonment.

> The proceedings concluded with the following exchanges between the officer in charge and Mr. Virag:
>
> Officer: Are you satisfied that the parade was conducted in a satisfactory manner and was fair?
> Virag:　I never was in Liverpool this year.
> Officer: Do you understand my question regarding the fairness of the parade?
> Virag:　Yes.
> Officer: Are you satisfied that the parade was fair?

Virag: Yes.
Officer: Have you any complaint to make regarding the parade?
Virag: No.

Mr. Virag then signed the appropriate form containing these questions and answers.

This passage concludes Appendix C of the Devlin Report and the official comment on it is an official silence. The discretionary status of rules governing judicial practice has been sufficiently spelt out in the rest of the report to require no further commentary in an appendix. Rules evolve historically as a result of judicial practice. Human error accounts for rule-breaking, and intellectual endeavour (research) accounts for rule-amendment.

The status of the rules defined   The recommendations of the Devlin Report concerned, first, a statutory change limiting a judge's discretion in regard to dock identification and requiring him to direct the jury more closely and specifically on identification evidence; second, two new codes; the Parade Rules and the Use of Photograph Rules. Yet although the Report gives primacy to normative explanation and normative reform it has to recognise that it is normative failure which has defined its object of inquiry. Therefore, the Report has again and again to define normative failure as being the unusual but natural result of human error (on the part of individuals in law-enforcement agencies) aggravated by the obduracy to normative regulation of that part of the population which is absolutely criminal. Thus in Dougherty's case a probationer policeman and his supervisory sergeant were found guilty of neglect of duty though it is stated (quite inaccurately) that 'a Chief Constable . . . recognised from the first that there were faults' (HC 338:28, para 2.64). In Virag's case the Report states that although there was a misjudgment in the Home Office, 'It is not our business to look for a culprit and we are therefore quite content to accept the view of his superiors that there was no incompetence or neglect'. The authorities however are now on the horns of a dilemma. Reluctant to ascribe blame to Home Office officials they have to consider with pained astonishment (and glimpses of the Unofficial Other must always generate astonishment) that the institution, the Home Office itself, is not all that it purports to be:

We cannot accept the view that the explanation lies simply in an individual error or judgment. The decision was substantially confirmed by the Senior Executive Officer. The decision and the confirmation of it are in themselves so astounding as to suggest the possibility of an error in the principles which are generally applied in the Home Office in such cases; we shall consider this possibility in Chapter Six.

In Chapter Six two reasons are given for the 'serious misjudgment' of the Home Office official: overwork due to staff shortage and erroneous application of principles. A remedy is sought by increasing ('reinforcing') the number of officials in the relevant department and by reiteration of the correct principle to be applied in similar cases in the future. Yet, throughout the Report it is stressed that rules are guides to, rather than determinants of, behaviour and the meanings given to it. The two dimensions of legal rules that are most often stressed are (1) practicality, i.e. they must not be such that too many 'guilty men' go free of punishment and (2) flexibility, i.e. that police and judiciary should be allowed enough discretion to ensure 'that there can be avoided on the one hand too severe a rigidity and on the other too wide a discretion' (HC 338: 127, para. 5.88). Here is the Golden Mean of the Common Law. The authorities consistently and didactically establish within Official Discourse the rectitude of its judicial mediators.

The rectitude of the judiciary Prerequisite and consequential to the establishment of the evolutionary development of judicial rule-usage is the establishment of the rectitude of the judiciary itself. Even when changes in the system *are* precipitated, judicial control of the timing and propriety of such change has to be reasserted. The Lord Chief Justice made this very clear when, after allowing Dougherty's appeal, he stated:

> We feel that that is as far as we can or should properly go today but the case has undoubtedly disclosed a number of matters which require urgent and careful consideration hereafter, *and that is a matter we must look after in our own way and in our own time* (ibid.: 28, para. 2.60. our emphases).

Not that the state is averse to incorporating and destroying the knowledges of those who might be its severest critics. Psychology and sociology all have a part to play in judicial mediation of the law – so long as the research team is carefully and officially chosen!

Referring to the need for further research into identification parades Devlin suggests that such research would require 'the participation not only of qualified psychologists but of the Home Office, the legal profession and the police' (ibid.: 73 para. 4.15). What has to be established is that the judiciary is still the only *authorised* interpreter of psychological and sociological research into judicial matters. Only the judge can mediate between scientist and layman, as the following passage from the Devlin Report makes clear:

> The juryman brings into the jury box his experience of everyday affairs, but the judge must, where it is necessary, reinforce that with the judicial experience derived from close contact with the administration of justice. Moreover, as Mr. Justice Moore pointed out, judicial experience is not static. It is to be obtained today not merely from work in court but also from sociological and psychological studies which a judge may be expected to read and a juryman would not (ibid.: para. 4.88. See also para. 4.81).

And so it goes on. Idealistic tautologising demonstrates the absurdity of the notion of mediation. The Judge, the authorities rightly claim, mediates the law correctly because he, like the policeman and any other state official, *is* the law.

The explanatory claims of Official Discourse are tautological, but their empiricist mode of exposition necessitates regular confrontation with the Other of the discourse. Appeals made to the normative common-sense knowledge of the knowing (and legitimated) subject of the discourse are nonetheless rooted in the material common-sense (the Symbolic) wherein lurks the Other. Appeals to normative common-sense, however, are always upheld by effecting predictions of future remedy as denials of present problems. Listen to the state talking to itself about class relationships as they affect identity parades:

> Disputes about the conditions for holding a parade are rare. The system works well enough at present by a combination *of reasonableness on the part of the police and fear on the part of the suspect* that lack of co-operation will prejudice his chances at the trial. This fear may be diminished by the restraints placed on dock identification: it may also tend to grow less with the spread of legal advice. The time may come when the suspect will appreciate – and act upon the appreciation – that he is no more

101

obliged to go on a parade without a solicitor, *or indeed under any other conditions which he dislikes*, than he is to make a statement without a solicitor (ibid.: 115, 5.40 our emphases).

In other words, the withering away of the state will be effected by the education of the working class. It will be an education which, like Official Discourse itself, paradigmatically denies the class relationships which both engender and destroy it.

The other paradigm

The paradigms and syntax of Official Discourse which establish the possibilities (or not) for future authoritative address also establish what is officially Unspeakable. On the Devlin Report's own evidence there was much that was unspeakable in the cases of Luke Dougherty and Laszlo Virag. On the Report's own evidence the immediate and major material causes of Dougherty's and Virag's wrongful convictions resided in the defendants' complete lack of credibility within and without the courtrooms. This complete lack of credibility was the effective product of the police, the legal profession's and the judiciary's effective relationship to working-class defendants. It is Unspeakable that we should suggest that the authorities should have looked more carefully at the descriptions of Dougherty's and Virag's class position and especially at how it defined their relationships with legal and judicial personnel. Yet it is to these descriptions that we must now turn. For in the Unspeakable (the Symbolic) resides the Other. The blow-by-blow accounts of 'what happened' in the cases of Dougherty and Virag revealed the following features which were never subsequently discussed as being even partially constitutive of the 'miscarriages of justice'.

1 *Both defendants found it difficult to assemble witnesses to support their alibis.* They found it difficult because they were hard-up (Dougherty had to take his witnesses to Court in a taxi) and because they lacked the powers of intimidation of the police (ibid.: 42, 3.37). In both Dougherty's and Virag's case their friends who could have supported their alibis were reluctant to enmesh themselves within the state's machinery of justice.

2 *Neither defendant was fully aware of his legal rights*; neither was very critical of his solicitor. Indeed it can be argued that Dougherty was pressured into retaining the same counsel against his own better judgment (ibid.: 25).

3 *Both defendants were out of work, and had been in trouble before*. Both gave a bad impression in court and while Dougherty especially was seen to be judicially incompetent, Virag was seen to be a foreign scrounger. The Devlin Report describes how Dougherty's counsel found him 'a difficult client' and notes that 'he was so concerned to protest his innocence that it was difficult to get him down to hard facts'. (!) Virag's background, Devlin implies, was so Unspeakable that it inevitably inhibited his defence counsel. Listen to the authoritative depiction of Virag:

> The picture of Mr. Virag that had by now inevitably emerged for the jury's inspection was that of a Hungarian refugee who lived on the social benefits which this country provides and spent his time gambling in a club where a brawl and a broken head were noteworthy as causing half an hour's interruption of play. It was not an attractive picture; and it might be thought that only a piece of clinching evidence would make it worthwhile offering to prosecuting counsel further opportunities of exploring life at the Trojan Club (ibid.: 50, 3.67).

In short both Virag and Dougherty were an embarrassment to their lawyers and more than once the Devlin Report stresses that solicitors and counsel acting for the men did well in the circumstances.

The antipathy of the jury towards Virag, the cursory way in which Dougherty was treated by the police and Virag by the Home Office are stated as part of the order of things by the Devlin Report. The discursive possibility that many more people like Dougherty and Virag are similarly crushed by the judicial machinery of state is pre-empted by the regularity with which the Report asserts that such miscarriage of justice is the exception rather than the rule.

We have so far only located the permitted and unpermitted parameters within and without which the Official Discourse takes place. In the remainder of the paper we will discuss the structure of their discursive presentation.

Syntax

Following Giglioli (1972) we are using the term syntagmaticity to refer to the sequential organisation of discourse, to the fact that utterances are connected in a meaningful way. We shall argue that the structure of discourse evidenced in these texts sustains a discursive regularity. In general terms, after the over-arching problem is stated a method of investigation is assumed. This method is the epistemology of judicial satisfaction that is supposedly arrived at through a positivist conception of an exhaustive investigation of the facts. This method constitutes and is constituted by a tautological discourse which assures that particular problems are assuaged through the manner of their posing. The discourse of tautology operates by a process of apposite history whereby the significant origin of a problem is proclaimed by fiat. Argument is structured through a form of narrative history which determines the central issues to be addressed – who started the riot?, was there any civilian shooting? . . . When the detailed problem has been formulated the knowing judicial subject attempts to appropriate the problem by a series of techniques of negation. However, these techniques allay the problem at a substantial cost. The manner in which the problem is dissolved necessitates the subject and object of the proclaimed discourse moving outside both the idealised conception of justice it speaks to and from and the supposed problematic that realises this conception. Both the subject and object of justice are displaced and the desire to reconstitute the ideal is exposed. The exposition of these discursive regularities will take the form of giving brief examples of the strategies used followed by a longer passage in which the techniques are overdetermined.

The knowing subject – and why he knows

The Scarman Tribunal's general problem was to make findings as to the causes of the breakdown in law and order which resulted in death, injury and destruction. This leads them to the judicial allocation of blame to Protestant or Catholic crowds. But they recognise that their problem was not only that law and order had broken down but that the agents of law and order had been the object of widespread condemnation for their activities in the riots:

> In a very real sense our inquiry was an investigation of police conduct. Criticism was directed against the higher direction of the RUC, the manner of their employment on the streets during the disturbances, the use of CS gas, the use of guns, and the behaviour of individual policemen (Cmd 566, 3.1).

Faced, accordingly, with the task of extracting evidence from the complexity of a riot situation and adjudicating between directly conflicting evidence the Tribunal asserts its judicial epistemology:

It will be observed that on some, but not all, of the matters referred to us we have made findings. We would only emphasise that we have considered ourselves entitled to make findings only in those instances in which we have felt sure we knew the truth (ibid.: 3 para. 8).

The epistemology of judicial satisfaction litters the text: 'Undoubtedly', 'We are satisfied', 'It has to be admitted', 'In our judgement', represent the typical introduction to the assertion of facts. Being in cognisance of the facts allows the knowing subject of the law to intervene in disputes about the essential meanings of material events:

The Tribunal has received a great volume of evidence dealing with the catastrophic riot that developed in the Ardoyne on the night of the 14th August. Very naturally the evidence contains inconsistencies, many of them irreconcilable and some of it is, the Tribunal believes, pure fantasy. While it is not possible to resolve all the conflicts and differences to be found in the evidence, the Tribunal is satisfied as to the principal features of the night's rioting. They were . . . (and 12 points are enumerated) (ibid.: 22.1).

Time and again the authorities proclaim their satisfaction and exercise their right to correct one witness, to overrule another and to make a finding of fact. This knowingness draws upon the stack of authority invested in the judicial site from which the knowing subject speaks. Official Discourse necessarily centres around a subject who assumes his entitlement to adjudicate. In answer to Foucault's primary question:

Who among the totality of speaking individuals is accorded the right to use this sort of language? Who is qualified to do so? Who derives from it his own special quality, his prestige, and from who in return, does he receive if not the assurance, at least the presumption, that what he says is true? What is the status of the individuals who – alone – have the right, sanctioned by law or tradition, juridically defined or spontaneously accepted, to proffer such a discourse? (Foucault, 1972: 50).

It is, in state discourse, justice incarnate, the object made man: The Hon. Mr Justice Scarman.

But the knowing subject does not only draw from his institutional site, he asserts a method: justice comes via truth. And the method in these judicial texts for access to the truth is the positivist conception of the thorough. Why the knowing subject knows is because: 'We have considered ourselves entitled to make findings only in those instances in which we have felt sure we know the truth' (Cmd 566, 8, para. 3). Knowingness is the product of the method of being absolutely thorough; the attempt is to recreate the totality of the event, to furnish an image of completeness which can serve to celebrate the image of authority. Thus the penchant for detail, the breadth and depth of the investigations, the sheer volume of the material received bear witness to the aspirations of judicial epistemology, namely post-factum recreation:

> The Tribunal was greatly assisted in its work by both solicitors and counsel it instructed to appear before it. But for the skilled and sustained work of both counsel and solicitors instructed on behalf of the Tribunal an investigation as complex and detailed as this inquiry proved to be could never have been completed. We are equally indebted to counsel and solicitors for those to whom we gave leave to be represented; their thorough cross-examination of witnesses and well prepared final submissions *illumined much that was obscure* and ensured *that a full hearing was given to all* affected by the inquiry (ibid.: p. 3 para. 10. our emphases).

The authorities design to give leave to other legal subjects to join in the prodding positivist search for the facts by 'illuminating' much that was obscure and ensuring a full hearing for all concerned. The Tribunal meticulously attempts to consolidate this method of the efficacy of facts through the sureness of its tone when dealing with the morass of detail it presents. On occasions it approximates to a video-tape replay:

> At 3.55 a.m. a series of explosions damaged the electricity sub-station at Castlereagh, some six miles from the centre of Belfast. Four charges of explosive were used, access having been gained by the removal of one of the railings so as to provide a gap through which a man could pass. A fuse tape was passed through the gap . . . (ibid.: 4.3).

The pre-given object – and how it is recognised

Official Discourse establishes the history of both the objects and subjects of that discourse as a *natural* history. In defining both the object of the discourse and its knowing constituents primacy is given to the natural evolution of rule-governed practices. Rule-governed practices are invoked to establish the absolute meaning of the evidence presented to the investigators, and this evidence has to be established as having a normative rather than a material history. Thus everything that 'happened' in the cases of Dougherty and Virag can be interpreted in terms of either past rule-usage or possible future rule-usage, but there is no possibility of explaining why *the evidence of the actual text* indicates that the rules in question were clearly not determinate of the current legitimation deficit. This absence is aggravated by the text's heavy reliance on the empiricist rhetoric of thorough and detailed factual description. Ironically, the product of this method as in the Scarman Report is a detailed account of material practices where primacy is given not to rules but to interprofessional and inter-class relationships. These relationships are presented both as having no history (because they are normatively intractable) and as being pre-historical (because they are rooted in human nature). That normative parameters of inquiry are the only legitimate and valid ones is established by the vocabulary of the first chapter of the Report.

The task of the first chapter of the Devlin Report is to provide the normative vocabulary which constitutes the lexicon for correct translation of the factual vocabulary of the following chapters. The vocabulary of chapter one, unlike the vocabulary of chapters two and three where named and particular events are presented as a series of contingencies evokes a world of 'time immemorial' (HC 338 p. 2) where things happen 'necessarily', 'normally' and 'inevitably'. The historical backcloth to the particular evidence under review is composed of policemen who have 'a natural desire for justice' (ibid.: p. 2) and a 'general notion that they should act fairly to everybody' (ibid.: p. 5), of judges who 'act as occasion requires, solving each problem as it comes along', and a 'criminal process weighted against conviction' (ibid.: p. 2). A passage on page 2 of the Report indicates how pre-history and human-nature are invoked to demonstrate the natural evolution of rule-governed practices which are thereby rendered inviolate.

If the police in making their enquiries act in a way which the judge at the trial considers to be oppressive and unfair he has *from time immemorial* exercised the power in extreme cases of excluding any evidence thereby obtained and in other cases of commenting adversely in a way that damages the prosecution's case. So that the police have had from the earliest time a motive, apart from *their natural desire for justice*, for ascertaining what standards the judges are likely to apply; and they have from time to time sought guidance from the judges themselves. This has led to the formulation of codes of conduct on various topics. The most celebrated of these codes is known as the Judges' Rules . . . (ibid.: p. 2: 1.8. our emphases).

With the location of the object of the practical discourse the knowing subjects of that discourse are simultaneously located. The object of the practical discourse has been defined in such a way as to render the subsequent empirical material immaterial; its knowing subjects are thereby established, and appealed to as men of normative (conservative) common-sense. But the legitimation deficit which engendered the discourse can not have been created by the objects and subjects of a normative common-sense. To account for the absent Other of the discourse two types of common-sense subject have to be depicted. First, there is the 'layman', the subject who too willingly accedes to the claims of the empiricist text, the subject who 'does not understand' that the material descriptions have to be translated into the normative vocabulary of the discourse's pre-given object. Second, there is the state's man who embodies the distilled but fully articulated socio-technicist knowledges of the state's normative history. As we will argue later, much of the syntax of the discourse is directed at covertly disarming and remedying the layman's radical common-sense, but the starkest and most overt example of the tension between the illegitimate and legitimate knowing subjects of the discourse is given on page 20 of the Devlin Report:

> 20 or 30 people in Sunderland now knew beyond a shadow of doubt that an innocent man had been sent to prison. What was their knowledge must soon be the knowledge of the whole neighbourhood and then the town, for the truth was easily ascertainable. . . . So that to a layman there seemed to be no reason why the truth should not immediately prevail. For the lawyer and administrator, however, the verdict of a jury is a solemn thing and cannot easily be disturbed.

The illegitimate knowledges of laymen provide the silent rationale for a discourse whose total structure has to translate that rationale within a paradigmatic and syntactic rationality which will destroy it. The paradigms are tautologies; the syntax attempts to negate all material evidence which would puncture this hermeneutic circle of idealist tautology.

The discourse of tautology

Within the overarching problem of the collapse of law and order the Scarman Tribunal addresses itself to particular problems that occurred in different places and times. It introduces the event, determines the core issues and makes a finding which attempts to allay the problem. It is in the manner of the posing of the particular problems that a discursive regularity is displayed. This process takes the form of asking and answering questions – were the riots a conspiracy? was this attack planned? who fired the first shots? Such issues become the central problems and thus, as well as displacing unasked questions, they simultaneously lead to a closing of the forms which the reply may take. Consider the questions the Tribunal asks about the Derry Apprentice Boys march that took place on 12 August 1969 and which precipitated the province-wide riots:

> Should he (the Minister for Home Affairs) have banned it? The question concerns the Tribunal only if the facts are such that it can be said that by refusing to ban it, the minister acted unreasonably. But should it be established that a neglect of duty by the Minister caused or contributed to the disturbances into which we are directed to inquire, the Tribunal must say so (Cmd 566: 10.3).

By 10.8 the issue has become even more refined:

> Was it possible in practice to impose a ban on the parade? Given the information which the Minister for Home Affairs had at the time, did he act reasonably? These are the two questions which must be answered before we would be prepared to criticise those who took what in the event proved to be a decision fraught with tragic consequences: and the answers can be given only after an examination of the course of events from mid-July to mid-August (ibid.: 10.8).

This lesson in methodology completed, the factual exercise is then

109

carried out and the adjudication proceeds:

> The Tribunal, therefore answers the two questions put as follows
> . . . (the ban could have been imposed in July but not August, the
> Minister underestimated to what extent the police had lost
> control in the city and the significance of the Derry Citizens
> Defence Association and overestimated the efficacy of the
> stewarding arrangements for the march). . . . But the decision to
> ban or not to ban was difficult, and, given the information and
> advice proffered to him, the Minister did not unreasonably in
> allowing the parade to proceed (ibid.: 10.18).

In its pristine form the discourse of tautology is achieved by three
stages of appropriation. The first concerns the theorising of a beginning, the second the structuring of an argument and the third its
attempted resolution.

The first we call apposite history. Here the problem is located in
the discourse by a form of narrative history that cuts off at particularly apposite moments. This asserts that the cut off point represents the significant origin of the problem. History is introduced and
managed as a stream of events which the Tribunal can enter into and
depart from at will in order to locate the problem under scrutiny:

> An accurate assessment of the 1969 disturbances requires some
> knowledge of events in the Province since unrest developed in
> 1968. These initial events have been described in the Report of
> the Cameron Commission, and we feel we can deal with them
> briefly. (ibid.: 1.2)

Continuity thus achieved, the apposite point to enter the stream of
Anglo-Irish history becomes:

> In June 1968 the local Member of Parliament (NI) exposed a case
> of discrimination in favour of an unmarried Protestant girl. The
> agitation which started over this case caught the imagination of
> the non-Unionist minority in the Province and greatly increased
> the standing influence of the Northern Ireland Civil Rights
> association. Events elsewhere in the world, particularly perhaps
> the student riots in France in the early summer of that year,
> encouraged the belief that a policy of street demonstrations at
> critical places and times could achieve results if only because they
> would attract the attention of the mass media. (ibid.: 1.3)

Thus are we thrown into the complex history of a sectarian state.

110

The discourse has now been located, the significant origin becomes 1968 (and in France!); starting has ended the past, but the past has been pulled into the present. Well might Foucault write:

> Continuous history is the indispensable correlative of the founding function of the subject; the guarantee that everything that has eluded him may be restored to him; the certainty that time will disperse nothing without restoring it in a reconstituted unity; the promise that one day the subject – in the form of historical consciousness – will once again be able to appropriate, to bring back under his sway, all those things that are kept at a distance by differences, and find in them what might be called his abode. Making historical analysis the discourse of the continuous and making human consciousness the original subject of all historical development and all actions are the two sides of the same system of thought (Foucault, 1972: 12).

The subject here is not historical consciousness but its mediated embodiment, the idealist theory of the state. The state in dealing with a problem locates the legitimacy deficit within its own narrative history – suitably cut off at apposite moments – while retaining the problem within the continuity of its past.

Once a problem has an origin, an argument is built around it which takes a guise of temporal neutrality. Construction of what is essentially an imaginary perspective appears as a natural emergent from the past. In the above example (1.3) the history of the beginnings of the disturbances moves on to trace the events of the 1968 October march in Derry, the subsequent riot and the reform programme. Narrative history exposes that it has, after all, an implicit perspective:

> Undoubtedly, the Government was faced with a dilemma. If it stood firm it attracted violent opposition. Yet to promise reform after the threat to law and order was a recipe to encourage further demonstration and counter-demonstration, and to increase rather than diminish the risk of confrontation between minority groups and the police (Cmd 566: 1.4).

There follows a little more 'history' (1.5) about the People's Democracy march in January 1969 and the rioting that followed in the Bogside. This is directly followed by the state again arguing its case: The reform programme had left opposition activists dissatisfied, but at the same time it had evoked hostility from some Protestants (ibid.: 1.6). 1.7 sees more history, 1.8 more argument:

> While the Catholic minority was developing confidence in its power, a feeling of insecurity was affecting the Protestants . . . In these circumstances sectarian conflict was to be expected unless the police were strong enough to prevent it.

The problem has been situated now both historically and in theory – in a position where it can be negated. But if the reader's suspicion has already been aroused that this narrative history, laced with implicit argument, is in breach of the positivist epistemology adopted at the outset his doubts will soon be confirmed. The techniques used to dissolve the problems thus posed sees the subjects and objects of the discourse being further displaced and transformed.

The techniques of negation

The particular problems threatening the state's legitimacy which the Scarman Tribunal confronts are enormous. They involve situations in which police are alleged to have: killed civilians through the use of indiscriminate and unwarranted force including gun fire; fired into unarmed crowds; connived with Protestant rioters; colluded in the destruction of Catholic property and stood in the way of inquiries into these allegations. The state is confronted with the task of accounting for these allegations within a paradigm that asserts the essentially just nature of the state, its practice and agents. Official Discourse seeks to neutralise these problems, to annihilate the Other while simultaneously affirming that justice has been done.

The most frequent line of argument adopted asserts that there were material reasons why the police deviated from accepted standards or why there was a more general non-performance of justice. These reasons acknowledge that there were just not enough police to cope with the breakdown or that the police were worn out. The idealised subject/object of justice is forced to recognise itself as justice within certain material conditions:

> (Belfast August 2nd) Two criticisms have been made of the behaviour of the police in Upper Library Street: First, that they made insufficient attempts to stop the stoning and the attack on

the flats by the Protestant crowd, and, secondly that one or more police officers threw stones at the flats . . . two parties of police did their best to keep apart an aggressive Protestant crowd of 200 and an equally determined group of residents within the flats. But, as so often, there were not enough policemen for the job they had to do. . . . After a full consideration of the evidence we have come to the conclusion that Constable Rainey did not throw stones. Mrs. Austin was mistaken, but, had the police been present in sufficient numbers to suppress Protestant stone throwing, it is likely that the accusation would never have been made (Cmd 566: 97.9).

Not only does the lack of resources account for the ineffectiveness of the police but also for the conditions in which allegations arise.

A second mode of negation places allegations in a context which invites the reader to understand not only how such complaints arise but also how they are mistaken. The Tribunal appeals to the 'honest but mistaken beliefs' which individuals adopt in riot situations. Appearances of what police action ostensibly looks like is shown to be an understandable but incorrect interpretation of real police motives. The authorities are, however, in the privileged position of being able to infer the real motives, plans and tactics of police activities. The example that follows concerns one of the many occasions when Protestant rioters followed the police into Catholic areas as they repelled a Catholic crowd: but things are not what they seem:

Derry 12/14 August. The Rossville Street incursion: What was its effect on the course of the riot? It must have hardened attitudes in the Bogside. The smashing of the barricade, the entry of the armoured cars and foot police, closely followed by Protestant civilians throwing stones, appeared to many as the physical embodiment of their worst fears. The fact that the police had in mind the limited tactical objective of relieving the pressure of rioters upon William Street, the fact that there was no concerted plan between police and Protestants, – these facts, though the Tribunal is completely satisfied as to them, were not evident to the people of the Bogside. They believed that they were witnessing an attack on them by the police and Protestants. The effect of it on Fr. Mulvey's mind was typical: thereafter there was 'complete unanimity in opposition to the police force' by a 'community in revolt' (ibid.: 11.29).

In this and on similar occasions, the Tribunal has moved beyond the positivist empiricism of appearances to employ a different order of fact: the facts of an empiricist subjectivism. The knowing subject of the law has shifted his criterion of 'satisfaction' to allow a knowledge that derives from the empathetic reconstruction of states of mind, opinions, meanings and the conditions which generate them. Thus displaced the authorities can proceed with their adjudication.

A third mode of negating an allegation is by recourse to common sense or natural reason (c.f. Devlin, section (ii) above). This strategy entails an appeal to a form of understanding that all addressed subjects can collude in. It is an understanding derived from everyone's everyday knowledge or an understanding given by the nature of the mind. This mode frequently takes the form of a quiet request which invites the reader to ponder on what he would have done in the circumstances. The logic of the technique is dependent upon a reasoning that presumes prescription – in these circumstances the likely, natural, understandable thing to occur did occur. Understanding is deemed to make explanation unnecessary. In Dungannon on 14 August armed 'B' specials (the police reserve) shot three unarmed Catholics. The Detective Inspector of the area attempted to find out who had been responsible for the shootings but all the Ulster Special Constabulary men on duty that day denied firing:

> The investigation proved inconclusive: the police officers concerned were not able to identify those responsible for the shooting. Some criticisms of the R.U.C.'s investigation were made before the Tribunal on the ground that it was not pursued with sufficient vigour. But this view ignores the very real difficulty which confronted the investigating officers. On the one hand they met with a complete denial of firing of all U.S.C. men on duty; on the other they were hampered by the unwillingness of some civilian witnesses to co-operate with them (Cmd 566: 14.50).

In these and other passages (e.g. 8.22, 9.27, 9.67, 12.23, 14.4) the problem under scrutiny is negated in the discourse by the invocation of an Other which displaces the idealised conception of justice espoused by the state. The knowing subject reappears as constrained by the materiality of the Other, as a knowing subject of empiricist intuitionism, or in the form of a collusive rationality that appeals to variants of common-sense. The positivist empiricism of the thorough which was to find by letting the facts speak for themselves has been dislodged.

These strategies still leave certain problems unresolved. Principally these occur when the Tribunal finds against the police – only to put in a plea of mitigation on their behalf. This type of fraternal critique admits of the transgression but emasculates any question of a legitimacy crisis by arguing that the breach was marginal. The image of justice has only been slightly tarnished. The example is again from Derry, again it concerns stone-throwing policemen:

> Fr. Mulvey, a fair-minded man condemned it; others more prejudiced than he, must have been driven by it to an even greater bitterness and hostility towards the police than they already felt. Such tactical respite which such police stone-throwing may have achieved was heavily outweighed by the hostility it provoked. Yet the dilemma of the police must in fairness be stated (they had not been authorised to shoot or to use C.S. gas, so they threw stones). In so doing they fell below the standards required of a disciplined force, and descended to the level of the rioters opposed to them, but their provocation was severe, their difficulties great and they lacked effective means to protect themselves or to disperse the riot. Responsibility for the July riots rests fairly and squarely upon hooligan elements in the Bogside. They began and developed the disturbance. The most that can be said against the police is that in some of their counter-measures they stepped beyond the shadowy line that distinguishes what is justified conduct in suppressing a riot from what is not (ibid.: 7.34–7).

In all there are six occasions where the Tribunal sees 'the police, by act or omission were seriously at fault' (3.7). Of these all but one (21.143 concerning the use of Shorland vehicles armed with Browning sub-machine guns in Divis Street 14–15 August) are accompanied with elements of a fraternal critique of mitigation. None, to our knowledge, were ever acted upon.

There remains one, much used, option. This is not to make a finding. This has the seeming effect of reaffirming the positivist intent to find only when the facts are evident. To leave a problem unresolved is unsatisfactory, but to do so on the grounds that it would be unfair conjecture to find in the face of doubt is a technique which re-establishes the boundaries of the authorities proclaimed problematic. Mr Francis McCluskey died in Dungannon on the

115

night of the 13–14 August following a police baton charge on a crowd. He was either batoned or knocked over by the retreating crowd:

> It was widely alleged that he had been batoned by police and that he was an inoffensive, elderly man who had been a victim of police brutality. The Tribunal received a great deal of evidence dealing with the death of Mr. McCluskey. Unfortunately the evidence was no longer fresh (taken as it was nearly two years after the event) . . . It is no part of the Tribunal's duty to cover confusion with conjecture: and no finding as to the cause of the injury is therefore made. The indications in the evidence are against the inference of excessive use of force: and no criticism to that effect is made of the police. The evidence of the pathologist supports the view that Mr. McCluskey was unfortunate to die: his initial concussion was unlikely to have been fatal, but unfortunately the fracture crossed an artery and tore it (ibid.: 8.23/4).

The strategies by which state discourse confronts and deals with the problems of its object are clearly overlayed in the texts. Extricating some of the discursive regularities from the text ignores the manner in which the syntax of a discursive formation 'overdetermines' a problem. To conclude this chapter we give an exemplar in which many, though not all, of the discursive regularities are evident. Here the method and strategies of Official Discourse twist, change and transform themselves in an effort to absolve the threat to the state's legitimacy. This exemplar is taken from an early chapter of the Scarman Report specifically concerned with the police:

> Undoubtedly (*judicial satisfaction*) mistakes were made and certain individual officers acted wrongly on occasions. But the general case of a partisan force co-operating with Protestant mobs to attack Catholic people is devoid of substance and we reject it utterly (*affirmation of the object*). We are satisfied that the great majority of the members of the RUC was concerned to do his duty . . . Inevitably, (*common-sense*) however, this meant confrontation and on occasions conflict with disorderly mobs. Moreover, since most of the rioting developed from action on the streets started by Catholic crowds, the RUC were more often than not facing Catholics who, as a result, came to feel that the

police were always going for them, baton-charging them – never 'the others' (*empiricist subjectivism*). In fact the RUC faced and, if necessary, charged those who appeared to them to be challenging, defying or attacking them. We are satisfied that, though they did not expect to be challenged by Protestants, they were ready to deal with them in the same way if it became necessary. The Shankill riots of the 2/4 August establish beyond doubt (*positivist empiricism*) the readiness of the police to do their duty against Protestant mobs . . . But it is painfully clear from the evidence adduced before us that by July the Catholic minority no longer (*apposite history*) believed the RUC was impartial and that Catholic and civil rights activists were publicly asserting the loss of confidence. Understandably (*natural reason, common-sense*) these resentments affected the thinking and feeling of the young and irresponsible and induced the jeering and throwing of stones which were the beginnings of most of the disturbances. The effect of this hostility on the RUC themselves was unfortunate (*natural reason*). They came to treat as their enemies, and accordingly also the enemies of the public peace, those who persisted in displaying hostility and distrust towards them (*common-sense*). Thus, (*argument through temporal neutrality*) there developed the fateful split between the Catholic community and the police. Faced with this distrust of a substantial proportion of the whole community and short of numbers (*material negation*) the RUC had (as some senior officers appreciated) lost the capacity to control a major riot. Their difficulties naturally (*natural reason*) led them, when the emergency arose, to have recourse to methods such as baton-charges, C.S. gas and gunfire which were ultimately to stoke even higher the fire of resentment and hatred.

Having posed the problem in terms of an understandable deterioration the Tribunal gives six occasions when they find the police seriously at fault:

The conduct we have criticised was due largely to the belief held at the time by many of the police, including senior officers that they were dealing with an armed uprising engineered by the IRA (*subjectivist empiricism*). . . . In dealing with an armed uprising the usual constraint on police conduct would not be so strong, while more attention would be naturally given to the suppression of the insurgents than to protection of people's lives and property

117

I

(*natural reason*). In fact, the police appreciation that they had on their hands an armed uprising was incorrect (*subjectivist empiricism*). . . . But there was a more fundamental cause for these failures. Police strength was not sufficient to maintain the public peace (*material negation*), but the Inspector General acted in August as though it was. . . . These criticisms we have made should not, however, be allowed to obscure the fact that overall the RUC struggled manfully to do its duty in a situation which they could not contain. Their courage, as casualties and long hours of stress and strain took their toll, was beyond praise; their ultimate failure to maintain order arose not from their mistakes, nor from any lack of professional skill, but from exhaustion and shortage of numbers (*fraternal critique*) (ibid.: 3.1–10).

The reading and writing of
Official Discourse

> To understand a film like *American Graffiti*, its reality and its
> pleasure, it is necessary to consider the logic of that contradiction
> which produces a position for the viewer but denies that
> production (McCabe, 1977: 66).

This book is the report of an investigation into a well-established
practice, the holding of, and reporting on, official inquiries into law
and order problems. The report has been presented as an analysis of
a discourse, as an archeology of the discursive practices of the state.
Three years ago, however, at the time of the book's inception,
discourse analysis was not the dominant theme of the project. Or,
rather, we would not have cited an interest in 'discourse analysis' as
the instigator of the complex of questions which engendered the
project. Nor can we now. The major concerns of the book are not
new. They have intrigued generations of thinkers. We have posed
them, initially, as three inter-related questions.

First: how useful are the epistemological categories of the
science/ideology dichotomy to attempts to characterise the knowledges produced by opaque and overdetermined social practices?

Second: Can the (theoretico/political) relationships between the
social relationships of specific social formations and the constitution
of subjectivities be theorised?

Third: What are the limits of theory?

Each of these questions is posed from an intellectual site
embedded in complexes of other questions, assumptions and
beliefs. The purpose of this chapter, therefore, is to discuss each of
these questions. In so doing we are mindful of two material facts of
discourse: on the one hand, that 'the fullest understanding of what I

119

"intend" my audience (if any) to believe or to do might give little or no indication of the meaning of my discourse'. (Chomsky, 1965) on the other, that at the time of writing we are condemned to write within discursive technologies which posit exchange between (somehow) constituted subjectivities as a dominant mode of sense-making.

In also reviewing the analyses of the official reports we attempt to assess, first to what extent they have helped reformulate the questions which we consider in this chapter, and second, the extent to which the questions which generated the analyses have themselves been transformed by the theoretical practices which the analyses both constitute and deny.

The science/ideology dichotomy

At the time when we began this book we had been deeply influenced by the powerful critiques of epistemology which were currently being developed and discussed by Marxist scholars (Althusser, 1971; Timpanaro, 1975; Hindess and Hirst, 1975). Our own interest could have been, (and most likely still can be) characterised as 'epistemological'. It was not 'epistemological' in the sense that we wanted to develop a technology which would guarantee some kind of 'truth', but rather, it was epistemological in the sense that we were interested in questions relating to the possibility of correctly characterising, recognising, and *using* 'scientific' as opposed to 'ideological' modes of knowing.

The definition of science which we worked upon as our starting point was a materialist definition: science, we assumed, is a knowledge which generates power over the natural world *independently* of the imaginary subjectivities wherein it is transmitted. This materialist definition of science is in opposition to the two types of idealism characterised by Timpanaro as 'the historicist and humanist idealism' and 'an empirico-criticist and pragmatic idealism,' (Timpanaro, 1975: 31) which assume of scientific knowledge *either* that it can be guaranteed by *or* that it can be tested independently of, the linguistic technologies within which subjectivities are realised both with and without necessary effects.

These definitions of materialism, science and idealism alone, however, were (even as starting-points) inadequate to the enterprise. The reports which we were studying had been produced at the behest of governments troubled by, and needing to understand (for

120

whatever purposes) the recurring law and order crises of a western capitalist society. We therefore needed to characterise the institutional and extra-discursive site of the reports' production. The theoretical characterisation which we gave to the institutional source of the reports was also pre-given within Marxist theory (Marx, 1967; Lenin, 1947; Althusser, 1971; Poulantzas, 1975a). We assumed, therefore, that these law and order reports had been produced within the state apparatuses and, further, that the role of the state apparatuses was 'to maintain the unity and cohesion of a social formation by concentrating and sanctioning class domination, and in this way reproducing social relations i.e. class relations' (Poulantzas, 1975a; 24). Thus, we had at the outset of the inquiry a materialist definition of science (though no protocol for its recognition) and a set of texts which, in the language of a recent but classically-inspired, historical-materialist exposition of class relations within the capitalist social formation (Poulantzas, 1975a), we characterised as productions of the state apparatuses. Once we had nominally located within theory the source of the official reports we were already working within a problematic of which the conditional object of inquiry was the theorisation of *practices* (rather than statements) in terms of their scientificity and/or their ideology. Beyond that moment, however, we knew not how to proceed. For the current critiques of epistemology, especially those of Hindess and Hirst, which we recognised as being pre-conditional to our present inquiry were also those which the inquiry, with its materialist assumptions, was condemned to question. We were unable to appropriate uncritically Hindess's and Hirst's work on scientific and ideological discourses because we ourselves were still partly working within a rationalist epistemology, as, we believe, in their *reaction* to epistemology, were Hindess and Hirst themselves. In recognition of this contradiction, that even in the critique of epistemology 'the already there-ness of instruments and of concepts cannot be undone or re-invented' (Derrida, 1976: 139) we attempted to operate both with a near-Bachelardian conception of science as developed by Hindess and Hirst *and* with a rationalist critique of that conception. We hoped that in practising a doubly negative approach we might produce new knowledge without closing off further inquiry within the inevitable (once specified) protocol of either position. (We assumed, of course, that independently of our 'attempts' or 'intents' the discourse of this text would establish both protocols and constituencies of readers.)

121

Soon after we began working on the official law and order texts, Hindess's and Hirst's book, *Mode of Production and Social Formation* was published. In it they claimed that in an earlier book, *Pre-Capitalist Modes of Production* they had made 'a radical, but by no means complete, break with works of Althusser and Balibar' (1977: 1). A concern of both books had been to challenge the epistemological discourses which claim that there is a 'relation of "appropriation" or "correspondence" of knowledge to its objects' (1977: 7). Neither the existence of objects nor the existence of social relations was denied; they were not in question. It was, however, strongly asserted (repeatedly in *Mode of Production* and subsequently in Cutler *et al.* 1977: 108) that 'epistemological doctrines have no necessary discursive effects.' Effects could only be specified within the political discourses of specific conjunctures. [In Chapter 4 of this book we gave a fuller exposition of this position, as we read it and as we adhered to it. But, as we have stated, we could not read the book according to its own negative protocol (we did not, for instance, obey injunctions to 'bracket off' certain questions!).] But the discursive practices of *Mode of Production*, in being partly constitutive of a new discourse, were also partly constitutive of absences in that discourse, of questionings about which the discourse that engendered them had to keep silent. These questionings related to the science/ideology dichotomy, to the production (or not) of subjectivities (see below) and to the limits of theory (see below). In the remainder of this section we will describe how our (still partly rationalist) conception of knowledge inseminated our readings of *Mode of Production* whilst, at the same time, the (self-denying) discursive protocol of *Mode of Production* raised even more questions about the theoretico-political usefulness of characterising discourses in general as being either 'scientific' or 'ideological'.

The dominant questions which *Mode of Production* posed for us thus related to the characterisation (individualisation) of discourses: how can discourses be read? how can discourses be written? These were questions about which *Mode of Production* was silent and necessarily had to be, for two reasons. First, because the usage of the word 'discourse' in that book was merely gestural, a substitution for the word 'theory', and second, because the discourse of *Mode of Production* is dependent upon the epistemologies from which it distances itself. True, Hindess and Hirst never deny that epistemologies have effects, they merely fail to theorise the possible conditions for epistemologies to have effects within *Mode of Production*. In effect, epistemological rationalism (suppressed) is the Other of Hindess's and Hirst's discourse. In its absence is constituted a protocol dictating how *not* to engage in theoretical work, a protocol which, even if (as Hindess and Hirst claim) is not *idealist*, is at least ideal in that 'it glosses over some of the discursive (in Foucault's sense) problems of specifying the effectivities of individualised discourses at different levels of theorisation and within differently specified discursive formations. Yet this silence enabled us to specify more clearly one object of our investigation. Agreeing with Hindess's and Hirst's rejection of epistemology's claims to guarantee general and predictable effects of posited correspondences of the relationships between concepts and the relationships between real-world objects, we were, nonetheless, committed (and this commitment will be explained in section 3 below) to the theoretical work of reading the official publications with the intent of theorising the possibilities and usefulness of the generalised categories 'ideology' and 'science'.

Can the (theoretico/political) constitution and effectivity of subjectivities be theorised?

This also is not a new question. It has been explicitly posed by Marxist and non-Marxist writers and has been immanent in a variety of theories and 'disciplines'. Assumptions about the constitution of subjectivities – variously and generally referred to as Man (!), human-nature, consciousness (true or false? determined or creative?) role or self (*the* question of social psychology: when is a role not a role? When it's a self!) – have been implicit or operative in all discourses. Within Marxism alone there are available several differing assumptions about the ways in which the discursive practices of 'skin-bound organisms' (Wilden, 1972) can be theorised. Most interpreters of Marx's work, somehow, (via various combinations of empiricism, materialism and rationalism) manage to describe the insertion of 'abstracted' concrete entities (persons) into conceptual systems which, through the power of a 'privileged' knowledge (and the use of 'privileged' there is not *necessarily* ironical) endow them either with the forms of consciousness *or* the social positions which they either employ or are constrained by in the real world. But few of these theorists were, until recently, concerned with the power-relationships between signifying practices and other social practices, although, now, within the discursive practices of recent theorists, especially Jacques Lacan, it can be seen why Volosinov, one of the few Marxists who *did* make this his major concern, was also a linguist with a deep interest in Freudian psychoanalysis. By the time we were attempting to 'interrogate' (or theorise a reading of) the government publications, we already had available to us the writings of Barthes, Kristeva, Lacan and Derrida, all of which were variously concerned not with voluntaristic *knowing* subjects but with speaking/spoken subjects overdetermined by the creativity of their constitutive discourses. Chapter two of the book described the attempts to appropriate to this project some of the metaphoric terminology of these writers. In one way, the 'eclecticism' of this procedure was a calculated risk, based on our theorising of the 'limits of theory'. But it also caused us analytic problems which were both constitutive of and beyond our theoretical discourse. Some of the problems were foreseen by us at the beginning of the project. (Indeed, whenever we sought temporary refuge in an Althusserian rationalism we were appalled at the profligacy of our theoretical abandonment!) But the problems of reading and writing an analysis of the government publications as instances of ideological practices were acute. In chapter three on Official Discourse and State Apparatuses we described some of the more recent attempts to theorise the relationship between economy and ideological, legal, and political relations. What we did come to realise, however, was that the problems of reading and writing discourses are closely related to the third major concern of this text, a concern with the limits of theory.

What are the limits of theory?

We have already mentioned with reference to the work of Hindess and Hirst that in *Mode of Production* they operated with a very narrow definition of 'discourse'. Indeed it is difficult to see why they used the word at all – except to distinguish their own 'theoretical' discourse from the work of the 'epistemologists'. Witness, however, their own explanation:

> Throughout this text we refer to theory as theoretical *discourse*, Why do we use this term? Theoretical discourse we shall define as the construction of problems for analysis and solutions to them by means of concepts. Concepts are deployed in ordered successions to produce these effects. This order is the order

created *by the practice of theoretical work itself*: it is guaranteed
by no necessary 'logic' or 'dialectic' nor by any necessary
mechanism of correspondence with the real itself. Theoretical
work proceeds by constant problematisations and reconstructions. Theories only exist as *discourses* – as concepts in definite
orders of succession producing definite effects (posing,
criticising, solving problems) – as a result of that order.
Theoretical discourse, like discourse in general, speaking and
writing, is an unlimited process. . . . The reason why discourse is
interminable is because the forms of closure of discourse
promised in epistemological criteria of validity do not work.
They are silent before the continued discourse of theories which
they can never correspond to or appropriate (Hindess and Hirst,
1977: 7–8).

This explanation raised problems which we posed as two further
questions: (1) if theoretical work proceeds (as it most likely always
has done) by 'problematising' and 'reconstruction' then how is such
work done outside of an epistemology which, even if not *guaran-
teeing* a theory at least provides *conditional criteria* for the recognition (and usage) of reconstructed theories as reconstructed
theories? (2) if theories 'only exist as discourses' then what is the
relevance of theory? i.e. why theorise?

Both questions were double-edged (and posed, incidentally,
from a place where we had no desire to be. In the mirror of our own
desire we glimpsed only too frequently the sarcastic grin of
Epistemology). On the one hand, these two queries questioned the
possibilities (or not) of *reading* discourses both within and without
the effects of their internal discursive practices. On the other hand,
they referred to the possibility of *writing* discourses both within and
without the discursive practices of the dominant modes of reading
and writing texts. We have already discussed these latter problems
at greater length in chapter two on Discourse Analysis; here we are
concerned with the more general question of the recognition and
theorisation of theoretical practice.

Hindess and Hirst displace the theory/politics problem in the
following way. Having set up a critique of a narrowly conceived
epistemology (i.e. epistemology as being that which *only* but *always*
and *forever* claims privilege as a knowledge form) they claim,
according to Gregor McLennan, that 'it is necessary to abandon
epistemology and determine the validity of arguments in terms of

internal coherence and the political/theoretical level of 'problem-
atisation' which the arguments aspire to' (McLennan, 1978).

> In political practice the conditions of calculation of effectivity
> and of the production of effect are separable. Political practice
> involves the *calculation of effect*, of the possibilities and results of
> political action, and that calculation rests on political relations
> which condition the degrees of certainty of calculation and the
> range of the calculable (Hindess and Hirst, 1977: 59).

Theoretical forms provide means for the calculation of effects and
the value of those theoretical forms is variable, dependent upon
political conditions. There is a silence about how the political conditions are to be theorised. At the limits of theory Hindess and Hirst
resort to metaphor, the only discursive practice explicitly available
to them at that moment in their work when they had: (1) denied that
they claimed any privilege for their own theorising; (2) reaffirmed
the existence of an extra-discursive realm of objects; (3) denied that
any specified relationships between the discursive and the extra-
discursive could be theorised; (4) denied that they are epistemological agnostics; and (5) denied that they are pragmatists. Gregor
McLennan (1978) sees the source of their (readers?) dilemma in
their catholic usage of the category 'epistemology' and suggests
that:

> By using a more limited version of epistemology, Hindess and
> Hirst can employ the following manoeuvre: our theory is not an
> epistemology nor a counter-epistemology, since we show that it
> avoids the pitfalls of all versions. There appears to be an
> important alternative posed at this juncture. (a) *Either* Hindess
> and Hirst must conform to what I have said is an idealist
> (coherency) position (this is terminological expediency, and not
> outright materialist condemnation!) *and in so doing* accept that
> their criterion of politico-theoretical problemisation is no more
> important than any other (including epistemological ones) or (b)
> they must concede that theirs itself is a position having
> epistemological and ontological significance, in which case the
> general argument fails (McLennan, 1978: 202).

McLennan argues that 'the latter alternative is the case' partly
because of 'the materialist premise of a socialist outlook which
Hindess and Hirst do not abandon' (McLennan, 1978: 202).
Although in *general* terms we would agree with McLennan we did at

that time, read into Hindess's and Hirst's discourse more of a promise (specification) of new forms of knowledge than can be conceived at the limits of their (or McLennan's) theorisation of epistemology.

At the limits of theory Hindess and Hirst could either have reappropriated (from epistemology) a theory of limits, or have displaced altogether their narrowly *conceived* concept of discourse. The discourse *itself*, however, sanctioned a third strategy, the resort to metaphor – before which theory remained silent. This is the discursive triumph of *Mode of Production*, the obstruction of the threatened theoretical closure. *Had* that closure occurred Hindess and Hirst would have been hoist with their own epistemology.

The above conclusion, that *Mode of Production*'s authorial claims were impotent before their discursive power, was not irrelevant to the question which had initially engaged us concerning the theory/politics relationship. But it transformed that question because it directed us to a new conception of theoretical work. *In its contradictions Mode of Production had destroyed the epistemological conditions of its existence but it had still made recognisable sense.* This theoretical discovery concerning *Mode of Production* was similar to what we had already suspected at a common-sense level about the official publications on law and order. We decided, therefore, to theorise 'discourse' in such a way that we might read Official Discourse and interrogate it as to the source of *its* discursive power. This text may have been a product of that analysis.

In the remainder of this chapter we will consider again the foregoing general questions but this time we will be both answering them and reformulating them in relation to the specific analysis of government publications. The first question concerns epistemology, the second concerns theory, the third is a question of the relationship between theory and politics.

The science/ideology dichotomy

Science and ideology cannot be dichotomised as polar opposites (except within untheorised discourses where they often refer to the crude dichotomies of: truth/not truth; with effect/without effect; direct experience/indirect experience; class-bound knowledge/non-class knowledge) because *as discourses* they constitute different orders of knowledge. Each discourse and each order of knowledge has different conditions of existence. These conditions of existence are specified in discourses which themselves have both theoretical and political conditions of existence. Consequential to this conception of archival *knowledges realised in discourse* is our assertion that epistemology has been displaced (though not destroyed) by discourse analysis.

By discourse analysis *in general* we mean to refer to the theoretical work which engages in a continuous *deconstruction* of a discourse. *In particular*, discourse analysis has to develop a theoretical protocol adequate to its theoretical object. (Below we discuss the discursive problems which we encountered in analysing the government publications within the protocol outlined in chapter two on discourse analysis). Here, however, we will be limited to summarising in general terms the implications for discourse analysis of the conceptions of science and ideology with which we were working.

'Science' was conceived in general but conditional terms as the theoretical moment of that effective power-relationship between social relations and discursive relations which produce new knowledge of the material world i.e. new conditions of existence for physical objects, social relations and knowledge effects.

'Ideology' was conceived in general but conditional terms as the theoretical moment of that effective power-relationship between social relations and discursive relations which both reproduces existent social relations *and* denies their extra-discursive conditions of existence.

Within the analytic discourse which we developed for the reading of the discursive texts of the government publications 'scientific' and 'ideological' referred in general to the values of the signifying practices. Those discursive practices which were theorised as being *potentially* preconditional to 'science' were those which were not, at least within the text, amenable to metonymic (ideological) closure. Those discursive practices which were theorised as being *potentially* preconditional to 'ideology' were those which, within the text, achieved closure. (In the final chapter of this book we summarize the textual modes of such closure.) what is *not* at issue therefore in discourse analysis is whether any particular discourse is rational (i.e. logically coherent) or not. What *is* at issue is first, how discursive effects are achieved (discourse analysis) and, second, a theoretico-political calculation of their value as signifying practices. It was in the theoretical context of these conceptions of the relationships between 'science', 'ideology' and 'discourse analysis' that we asserted that discourse analysis has displaced epistemology. These conceptions of science, also, are in opposition to all conceptions of science which lay claim to a scientific knowledge evolving under the sign of a privileged methodology forever proof against discursive attack, and which 'allows us to imagine that knowledge can exist only where the power relations are suspended and that knowledge can only develop outside its injunctions, its demands, its interests' (Foucault, 1977: 27).

The production of new knowledge does not depend on theoretical work alone. Discourse is conditioned within discourse in a layered metonomy of linguistic economy. At any specific conjuncture 'new knowledge' can be embedded in discourses where the knowledge-effect is but one amongst many others and where its power-effect is metonymised as a yet untheorised Other. At the same time, within the arbitrary boundaries of any specified discourse, subsist also the fractured constituents of an Other which mitigates *against* closure.

Finally, the politico-theoretical conception of how new knowledge-effect is achieved prohibits the notion of science as the essential property of an epistemologically privileged élite, class or class fraction. At any specific moment, however, a professional élite, a particular class or fraction of a class may be claiming monopoly of particularly effective discursive techniques. It is when a particular fraction of a class is both claiming epistemological privilege *and* is in effective control of the technical production of certain discourses in general and in explicit control of certain texts in particular (as in the case of the government publications) that it is most important, *in the interests of a politico-theoretical conception of science*, that a discursive deconstruction of those texts should be made. The most acute problem with which we were confronted was the problem of constructing a mode of deconstruction appropriate to the government publications.

Can the (theoretico/political) constitution and effectivity of subjectivities be theorised?

The postulate of tautology simply means that on the same page the same word must retain the same meaning. If one comes to use the word in a new sense, and if the context is not sufficiently clear so that the metaphorical meaning is evident, one must explicitly indicate the semantic change. The principle of tautology governs everything; even the imaginary, the fantastic, the unreal. It keeps the agreement constant between the author and the reader. It is the basis of reading.

But the permanence of the meaning of a word and the permanence of the properties of a thing have nothing in common. One must, therefore, distinguish between the postulate of tautology which affirms the permanence of the word and the postulate of identity, or more exactly the permanence of a characteristic or of a group of characteristics of an object (Bachelard, 1940: 98).

We have had great difficulty in posing the question which attempts to identify the major problem we have had in reading and writing *Official Discourse*. Correctly posed within a *Marxist* theory the question would have referred to the relationship between an economic base and an ideological superstructure. Correctly posed within *psychoanalysis* the question would have referred to the acquisition of a subjective language. Correctly posed within a 'pure' semiotics (though one rejected by Kristeva, 1975: 52) the question would have refused to countenance the possibility of even an interrogative linking of the discursive and the extra-discursive. Undoubtedly the question is not correctly posed. Positioned correctly, the object of the enquiry could never have existed. Specified in a metalanguage the object was always under an erasure. The lines within which we desired to write tantalised us with the self-denial of a presence which threatened closure. They tantalised us with an absence which threatened loss of meaning. Recognition of a desire to specify the 'ideological' within the government texts was the contradiction within which *Official Discourse* had to be read and written. It was the Other which punctuated both the reading and the writing of *Official Discourse*. But it was also an Other which we did not appropriate then and cannot now. What we will do instead is comment on some of the discursive strategies of the foregoing discourse and discuss some of the analytic problems which they pose.

As we described in Chapter 2, discourse always presupposes an addresser and an addressee, someone who speaks, someone who is addressed. We have argued, however, that the authorial power which presupposes an addressee is a creation rather than the creator of the text. Yet although we have attempted to analyse the government texts as a discourse on law and order we have at the same time held to a Marxist theory of the state apparatuses which, at a different level of theory, specifies that it is within institutional sites that Official Discourse is invested with the metaphoric power which, fractured beyond recognition, becomes the metonymic power of the text. At the same time we have not argued that there are direct causal links between discursive effects and extra-discursive social relations. They have different conditions of exist-ence and those conditions of existence have been specified within several different and contradictory discourses. This was the major problem confronting us in writing *Official Discourse* and we are not entirely convinced of the theoretical propriety of the discursive strategy whereby we confronted that problem.

The main discursive strategy used to write the contradictions occasioned by questions which were posed from within at least three contradictory discourses was metaphoric. In Chapter 2 we out-lined how we constructed an elaborate metaphor to write the theorised relationships between the (intra-discursive) articulations of signifiers and signified and the (extra-discursive) institutional sites. Within that metaphoric *bricolage* we attempted to reassemble the dominant signifiers (i.e. received knowledges, histories, subjects) and to describe the mode of their dispersion and punctua-tion within the text. But the 'metaphoric' strategy has had at least two ideological implications for the reading and writing of *Official Discourse*. First it has closed-off (or glossed over) questions concerning the protocol for assessing the internal coherence of *Official Discourse*. Second, it has raised questions concerning discourse analysis's relevance to theoretically informed political practice.

The reiterated arguments of this book have repudiated the notion of guaranteed theory, of a privileged theory which has necessary effects beyond the discourse in which it is realised as one effect amongst others. But these arguments have not repudiated the notion that all theory is written and read within existing protocols which it is condemned both to conform to (in the ordering, elabora-tion and refinement of the concepts) and to violate (in the metonymic effects of the texts). In Chapter 2 therefore we specified the concepts we were using both in terms of their *placement* (in other theoretical schemes) and their *displacement* within *Official Discourse*'s. We argue, therefore, in reply to possible charges of relativism or idealism, that the coherence (or not) of *Official Discourse* depends upon a metonymic logic, which, in maintaining a gap between the originary and displaced meanings of its conceptual apparatus, specifies what is *Official* about Official Discourse. This argument we think answers the epistemologist's charge of relativism, though we are certainly not saying that all discourse analysis should proceed by way of metaphoric deconstruction. We *are* saying that at the *limits of theory* it may be more important to communicate a contradiction by metaphor than to negate the contradiction by theoretical appropriation.

The specific metaphoric discourse within which we were writing also enabled us to answer the questions about authorship in terms which specified 'Author' as creation rather than creator of the text. This was a correct specification in terms of the linguistic theory which informed the discourse analysis but we were uneasy about the theoretical and political implications of this.

At a theoretical level we foresaw complaints that we had translated the 'real' authors into 'determined' authors positioned within the state apparatuses and 'functionally' producing state propaganda. We think that this criticism would be misplaced: first, because we claim no necessary relationships between discursive effects and any discursively attributed subjectivist intent; second, because the 'desire' which we use metaphorically does not refer to the 'intents' or 'wishes' of any individuals but to the objective political conditions which have to be maintained, repaired, renewed or reformulated if the state is to survive continuous crises of hegemony. Nevertheless there remains a certain ambiguity as to whether *Official Discourse's* specification of those discursive conditions is coherently achieved within the foregoing analytic texts or whether (contradictorily) their discursive specification was pre-given at the moment when the reports of the official inquiries were theorised as being instances of ideological practice within the state apparatuses. If the latter is the case then there has been a certain failure of theoretical practice in the writing of this text.

Beyond this point we cannot comment on the coherence or not of the text. Frank Kermode (1967) once wrote that 'it is a great charm of books that they have an end.' But that end is also a beginning, a beginning of the continuous rewriting of the texts by their readers. For it is a great charm too of books that they have their critics, addressees who, already existent within the text, render irrelevant that 'reflexive' Narcissism which some recent theorists have recommended as a final but already futile bid for authorial power. This text, arguing that theoretical work is just *one* (though essential) precondition for the production of scientific knowledge, claims too that the most acute dilemmas for a theorist (as opposed to a theoreticist) are not those of conceptual coherence but those theoretico/political dilemmas which exist *at and beyond the limits of theory*.

The limits of theory

The analytic mode of *Official Discourse* provokes at least two major theoretico-political questions. The first concerns the relevance of discourse analysis to a theoretically informed political practice. The second concerns language.

At a common-sense level the political relevance of discourse analysis was abruptly stated by Anthony Wilden in 1972 (XXVIII). 'You must know what your enemy knows, why and how he knows it and how to contest him on any ground.' Already, in 1968, however, Foucault (English translation 1978) had encountered and confronted the specific fear that, as a theoretical practice, discourse analysis could have an inhibitive effect on theoretico-political practice. The following question had been put to Foucault by the editors of *Esprit* after the publication in 1966 of his book *The Order of Things*.

> Doesn't a thought which introduces discontinuity and the constraint of a system into the history of the mind remove all basis for a progressive political intervention? Does it not lead to the following dilemma:
> —either the acceptance of the system,
> —or the appeal to an uncontrollable event, to the irruption of exterior violence which alone is capable of upsetting the system?

Foucault's reply consisted of a restatement of his project. This reply displaced the ontological assumptions of the question. The assumption of system-determinacy was displaced by a restatement of the implications of (what we have called) the indeterminacy principle of overdetermined events.

> The question which I ask is not that of codes but of events: the law of existence of the statements, that which has rendered them possible – them and none other in their place: the conditions of their singular emergence; their correlation with other previous or simultaneous events. This question, however, I try to answer without referring to the consciousness, obscure or explicit of

133

K

speaking subjects; without relating the facts of discourse to the will – perhaps involuntary – of their authors (Foucault 1978: 14).

Subsequently he was to pose the series of questions which stand as a rebuke to those who would wish *their* theoretical work to guarantee *them* a place in history:

> Is a progressive politics linked (in its theoretical thinking) to the themes of meaning, of origin, of the constituent subject. . . . Is a progressive politics bound to such a form of analysis—or with its being challenged? And is such a politics bound to all the dynamic, biological, evolutionary metaphors through which one masks the difficult problem of historical change – or on the contrary, to their meticulous destruction . . . must one think that a progressive politics is linked to the devaluation of discursive practices, in order for a history of the mind, of conscience, of reason, of knowledge of ideas or opinions to triumph in its certain ideality? (Foucault, 1978: 19).

The emphasis is again upon discourse analysis as a material practice which attacks and destroys. At the limits of (known) theory the concern is not with theoretical rectitude but with discursive effect. Discursive attacks will be made both within and without the protocols (rationalities and rules) of existent knowledges, but the rectitude of the theoretical procedures will not guarantee the product (nor vice versa). Conversely, however, the knowledge effect, if it is 'scientific' will both challenge the rectitude of the theoretical procedures *and* seek recognition within the destruction of their limits.

Foucault's contribution has been to displace the so-called human sciences' idealist and reactionary concern with the control of subjectivities. The theorist, now at the limits of theory, is displaced from the centre of the text and becomes one practitioner amongst many committed to the never-ending task of knowing-through-discursive-deconstruction, the material constitution of all social practices whether they be wholly discursive or predominantly non-discursive.

> What is in question is not an 'uninteresting terminological' process but the necessary social process through which the materialist enterprise defines and redefines its procedures, its findings and its concepts, and in the course of this moves beyond one after another 'materialism'. There are only two real barriers to this continuing process: one, ... of mythologising or

recuperating to received presumptions all that which we do not yet understand or understand imperfectly; the other, closer to home, of seeming to know in advance, and as a test of our political fidelity, the changing materialist content of materialism (Raymond Williams, 1978).

It is more easily said than done. How many exhortations! How few analyses! But even 'saying' discourse analysis is not easy. There remains the problem of language. This is a problem rooted both in the contradictions of the discursive project *and* in the social relations of societies still dominated by idealist and empiricist discourses reproduced within elitest education systems where competing fractions of the bourgeoisie struggle to retain institutional control of coercive linguistic technologies.

In this text we have repeatedly attempted discursive affirmation of a conception of science which, though not denying them, says 'No' to its own conditions of existence. Yet, within discourse, 'scientific' value is conferred via signifying practices conditioned by prevailing linguistic forms. But the analytic discourse has continuously to put under erasure what is signified in the name of signifiers existing beyond, and having no identity in, the discourse. The consequent discursive problem can be put quite simply: analytic discourses which attempt to violate the linguistic conventions within which they write more often than not (and it is unlikely that this text will be an exception) violate them to such an extent that the analytic discourse is itself difficult to the point of unintelligibility. How, it is often asked, can such difficult discourses claim to have political effects? (The *short* answer is that *whether it be intelligible or not, analytic* discourse cannot make such claims). More specifically, the interrogation continues, is it not ironic that *this* text – a text which in its very work of deconstruction affirms the ideological and comprehensive plausibility of government publications – cannot itself effect a more comprehensible mode of discursive attack? (The short answer is that, yes, it is ironic). These questions, both implying that the political effects of a discourse are reducible to positivistic discursive technique, require further comment.

Althusser, Foucault and Kristeva all conceive of discourse as a struggle in the realm of theory, though it is Althusser alone who sometimes slips into the error of implying that it is a failure of *will* on the part of his readers when they do not understand his texts. Both Kristeva and Foucault argue, however, that discursive struggle is necessary to the destruction of the subjectivist fallacy which locates meaning in the 'intersubjectivity' of 'author' and 'reader'. Kristeva (1975: 73), moreover, explicitly warns 'those committed to a practice of challenge' *against* the frequent temptation to 'Abandon their discourse as a way of communicating the logic of that practice'. Foucault is less patient with theorists who, now under the signs of 'democratic communication' and 'progressive politics', once more attempt to claim authorial control over the effects of a discourse: 'they do not want to lose *what they say*, this little fragment of discourse' (Foucault, 1978: 26). But they *will* lose what they say and neither the intelligibility (or not) of the discourse, nor its legitimacy (or not) nor its accessibility (or not) remain in authorial control. This is *not* to say that this work has been done without regard to the constraints of theoretical protocols, nor is it to claim that the analytic text is beyond critical evaluation. It *is* to say that the theory of discourse within which we write allows us neither *privilege to be within* nor *licence to stand without* the discursive effects of the text.

The rationale of discourse analysis is deconstruction of the known within the known. What is produced in that deconstruction cannot be retained and identified within that specific discourse. At the limits of theory there is no sovereign language which will guarantee meanings independently of the discursive and non-discursive effectivities in which the order of language is constantly renewed.

8 Official Discourse:
report of an unofficial inquiry

Official reports on inquiries into matters of official concern about law and order are written for public consumption. Above all, a judicious picture of the world is given. In the appeal to common-sense adjudication all sides of a question can be presented. *Any* view-point is eligible for consideration and *incorporation* (though not for *explanation*). Stalin (1973) recognised this when he insisted that language can serve all classes and that there is no class language as such. Clarke *et al.* (1977) however, have claimed that 'one further aspect of juridico-political ideology through which the capitalist state presents itself as a popular state standing above all classes is that "all traces of class domination are absent from its language."' (Poulantzas, 1975). On the contrary, we argue that the language of class domination is quite openly employed in official publications, and we conceive of no theoretical reason why any specific concepts or modes of argument should *per se* be unsuitable for incorporation into any already existent discourse. We agree more nearly with Volosinov (1976: 100) who argues that discourse 'does not at all reflect the extra-verbal situation in the way a mirror reflects an object. Rather the discourse . . . *resolves the situation*, bringing it to an evaluative conclusion.' What can be said or written, therefore, depends not so much on some pregiven and coherent ideology – be it juridical or political – but upon the discursive practices diachronically invoked to create an *apposite history*, and synchronically and arbitrarily used (cf. Saussure, 1974) to capture a *future convention*. To that latter extent, therefore, judicial discourse has formal characteristics which it shares with any discourse. When, however, it is incorporated into Official Discourse it is partly constitutive of a space which has to be closed effectively . . . but not

137

forever. For an Official Discourse, like the common-law and the common-sense, recognises that the conditions for reproductive change do themselves change. The official vasectomy has to have promise of its own reversal when the material situation changes. Until then – an effective operation is effected by the *Judicial stare*, an immaculate contraception for an illegitimate official desire.

Official Discourse on law and order confronts legitimation deficits and seeks discursively to redeem them by denial of their material geneses. Such denial establishes an absence in the discourse. This absence, the Other, is the silence of a world constituted by social relations the reality of which cannot be appropriated by a mode of normative argument which speaks to and from its own self-image via an idealised conception of justice.

The legitimated paradigms of the Discourse select from the discourses within which common-law, natural law and legal positivism have their rationales. Uniting natural law and common-law in a Hegelian conception of the state, they establish that legal rules inevitably evolve to meet the needs of the time and that their legality is guaranteed by the legitimacy of the state. This legitimacy of the state emanates from the intersubjective space where Lawgiver and knowing subject inhabit the temples of natural reason. The composite product of natural law theory and common-law theory is guaranteed by the rhetoric of legal positivism. The message of Official Discourse is that legitimation crises are precipitated by a normative lag aggravated by human fallibility, particularly the legal incompetence, lack of education and lack of social credit of the working-class.

The syntax of the discourse has to elevate the legitimated paradigms of the state and its justice at the same time as it suppresses alternative paradigms. Yet, despite the sophistication of its paradigmatic and syntagmatic structure, Official Discourse is unable to establish a theoretical discourse within which new knowledge of the non-discursive events which occasioned it can be gained. For the ideological metonymies of Official Discourse are directed not only to the destruction of their real conditions of existence but also, through denial of those conditions of existence, to their partial and surreptitious reproduction. To this extent Official Discourse is always directed at discursive closure. But the Other constantly obtrudes, demanding a recognition at the limits of discourse. The official publications which we studied, however, cannot confront and explain the real social relations which engender them. And the

Other, though denied, continues to effect a discursive demand – a demand which, once appropriated by the Official Discourse, can never be satisfied. In denying the Other, therefore, Official Discourse is condemned to constant, tautologous and Narcissistic assuagement of an impossible desire – the desire both to reconstitute and deny within discourse the real conditions of its existence.

Within the texts we read, the discursive struggle between the Official and the Unspeakable is instanced at the limits of *empiricism*. Empiricism is the chosen method of investigation. Empiricism proclaims that its logic depends upon a separation of subject and object. Yet Official Discourse re-presents its knowing subjects and known objects as a unitary whole. Again, the Other is to blame. Constant fracturing and realignment of its own epistemologies enables the state to guard against one of the dangers of empiricism, namely, that the descriptions necessary to empiricist rhetoric also provide the empirical evidence necessary for reconstitution of the Other. When the Other threatens to intrude in this way, the authorities, having already established that the subject and object of the discourse are at one, remedy the texts' legitimation crises by celebrating a subjectivist empiricism. This subjectivist empiricism in its turn establishes an apposite historical consciousness constituted by the ideal state's men, incarnations of an ahistorical and prehistorical justice. Within this tautological discourse are actualised the legitimate and illegitimate knowledges of the state.

Bibliography

ALTHUSSER, L. (1970), *Reading Capital*, London, New Left Books.

ALTHUSSER, L. (1971), *Lenin and Philosophy and Other Essays*, London, New Left Books.

ALTHUSSER, L. (1976), *Essays in Self Criticism*, London, New Left Books.

ARMOUR, L. and SAMUEL, G. (1977), *Cases in Tort*, Plymouth, Macdonald & Evans.

BACHELARD, G. (1940), *The Philosophy of No* (Trans. G. C. Waterson) London, Orion Press.

BARTHES, R. (1975), *Pleasure of the Text*, London, Jonathan Cape.

BARTHES, R. (1977), *Image, Music, Text* (Trans. S. Heath) London, Fontana.

BENVENISTE, E. (1971), *Problems in General Linguistics*, University of Miami Press.

BODENHEIMER, E. (1969), 'A Neglected Theory of Legal Reasoning', *Journal of Legal Education*, 21 373.

BURTON, F. and CARLEN, P. (1977), 'Official Discourse', *Economy and Society*, 6 (4): 377–407.

CAIN, M. (1976), 'Necessarily Out of Touch: thoughts on the social organisation of the Bar', in Carlen (1976).

CAMERON (1969), *Disturbances in Northern Ireland: The Report of the Cameron Commission*, Cmd 532, Northern Ireland.

CARLEN, P. (1976), *Sociological Review Monograph (23): The Sociology of Law*. Sociological Review, University of Keele.

CARTWRIGHT, T. (1975), *Royal Commissions and Departmental Committees in Britain*, London, Hodder and Stoughton.

CHOMSKY, N. (1965), *Aspects of the Theory of Syntax*, Massachusetts Institute of Technology Press, Cambridge, Mass.

CLARKE, J., CONNEL, I. and McDONOUGH, R. (1977), 'Misrecognising Ideology: Ideology in Political Power and Social Classes' in *Working Papers in Cultural Studies*, 10, Centre for Contemporary Cultural Studies, University of Birmingham.

CLOKIE, H. M. and ROBINSON, F. W. (1937), *Royal Commissions of Inquiry*, California, Stanford University Press.

CORY, W. (1882), *A Guide to Modern English History*, Part II, London, Kegan, Paul & French.

COWARD, R. and ELLIS, J. (1977), *Language and Materialism*, London, Routledge & Kegan Paul.

COX, B., SHIRLEY, F. and SHORT, M. (1977), *The Fall of Scotland Yard*, Harmondsworth, Penguin.

CULLER, J. (1976), *Saussure*, London, Fontana.

CUTLER, A., HINDESS, B., HIRST, P. and HUSSAIN, A. (1977), *Marx's Capital and Capitalism Today*, Vol. I, London, Routledge & Kegan Paul.

DERRIDA, J. (1970), 'Structure, Sign and Play' in Macksey, R. and Donato, E., *The Languages of Criticism and the Sciences of Man*, London, Johns Hopkins Press.

DERRIDA, J. (1976), *Of Grammatology* (trans. Gayatri Chakravorty Spivak), London, Johns Hopkins Press.

DIPLOCK (1972), *see* HMSO (1972a).

DOUGLAS, W. O. (1964), 'Stare Decisis' in *Essays on Jurisprudence from the Columbia Law Review*.

DUNCANSON, I. (1976), *Legal Positivism as Ideology*, unpublished paper, University of Keele.

DURKHEIM, E. (1957), *Professional Ethics and Civic Morals*, London, Routledge & Kegan Paul.

DURKHEIM, E. (1964), *Rules of Sociological Method*, New York, Free Press.

ENGELS, F. (1962), *Anti-Duhring*, Moscow, Progress Press.

FEYERBEND, P. (1975), *Against Method*, London, New Left Books.

FINER, S. E. (1952), *The Life and Times of Sir Edward Chadwick*, London, Methuen.

FINER, S. E. (1969), *The Transmission of Benthamite Ideas*, in Sutherland (1969).

FOUCAULT, M. (1972), *The Archaeology of Knowledge*, London, Tavistock.

FOUCAULT, M. (1974), *The Order of Things*, London, Tavistock.

FOUCAULT, M. (1977), *Discipline and Punish*, London, Tavistock.

FOUCAULT, M. (1978), 'Politics and the Study of Discourse', *Ideology and Consciousness*, Spring 1978 (3).

FRANKFURTER, F. (1964), 'Some Reflections on the Reading of Statutes' in *Essays on Jurisprudence From the Columbia Law Review*.

FREUD, S. (1976), *The Interpretation of Dreams*, Harmondsworth, Penguin.

FRIEDMANN, W. (1964), 'Legal Philosophy and Judicial Lawmaking' in *Essays on Jurisprudence from the Columbia Law Review*.

GIGLIOLI, P. (1972), *Language and Social Context*, Harmondsworth, Penguin.

GRAMSCI, A. (1971), *Selection from the Prison Notebooks*, London, Lawrence & Wishart.

GRAVE, S. A. (1967), 'Common Sense', *Encyclopaedia of Philosophy*, vol. 2, London, Macmillan.

HABERMAS, J. (1976), *Legitimation Crisis*, Boston, Beacon Press.

HAIN, P. (1976), *Mistaken Identity*, London, Quartet.

HALL, S., CRITCHER, C., JEFFERSON, T., CLARKE, J. and ROBERTS, B. (1978), *Policing the Crisis*, London, Macmillan.

HARRIS, Z. (1963), *Discourse Analysis Reprints*, The Hague, Mouton.

HEGEL, G. (1962), *Philosophy of Right*, Oxford University Press.

HINDESS, B. (1977), *Philosophy and Methodology of the Social Sciences*, Brighton, Harvester Press.

HINDESS, B. and HIRST, P. (1975), *Pre-Capitalist Modes of Production*, London, Routledge & Kegan Paul.

HINDESS, B. and HIRST, P. (1977), *Mode of Production and Social Formation*, London, Macmillan.

HIRSCH, J. (1978), 'The State Apparatus and Social Reproduction: Elements of a Theory of the Bourgeois State', in Holloway and Picciotto (1978).

HIRST, P. (1976a), *Problems and Advances in The Theory of Ideology*, Cambridge University Communist Party.

HIRST, P. (1976b), 'Althusser and The Theory of Ideology', *Economy and Society*, vol. 5 no. 4.

HMSO (1965), *Report of Inquiry by Mr A. E. James, Q.C. into the Circumstances in which it was possible for Detective Sergeant Harold Gordon Challenor of The Metropolitan Police to continue on duty at a time when he appears to have been affected by the onset of mental illness* (Cmnd 2735).

HMSO (1969), *Report of the Advisory Committee on Police in Northern Ireland*, Cmd 535. (Northern Ireland) Chairman, Hunt.

HMSO (1972a), '*Report of the Commission to consider legal procedures to deal with terrorist activities in Northern Ireland*' (Cmnd 5185 – Chairman, Diplock).

HMSO (1972b), *The Report of the Tribunal of Inquiry into Violence and Civil Disturbance in Northern Ireland in 1969* (Chairman, Scarman), Cmd 566, Northern Ireland.

HMSO (1975), *The Distribution of Criminal Business between the Crown Court and Magistrates' Courts*, Cmd 6323.

HMSO (1976), *The Report of the Secretary of State for the Home Department of the Departmental Committee of Evidence of Identification in Criminal Cases* (HC 338 Chairman, Devlin).

HMSO (1977), '*Report of A Court of Enquiry under Rt. Hon. Lord Justice Scarman, OBE into a dispute between Grunwick Processing Laboratories Ltd. and Members of the Association of Professional, Executive, Clerical and Computer Staff*' (Cmnd 6922).

HOLLOWAY, J. and PICCIOTTO, S. (1978), *State and Capital*, London, Edward Arnold.

HOOK, S. (ed.) (1964), *Law and Philosophy*, New York University Press.

KERMODE, F. (1967), *The Sense of an Ending*, Oxford University Press.

KRISTEVA, J. (1975), 'The System and The Speaking Subject', in T. A. Sebeok, *The Tell-Tale Sign*, Peter de Ridder Press.

KUHN, T. (1970), *The Structure of Scientific Revolutions*, University of Chicago Press.

LABOV, W. (1972), *Language in the Inner City*, University of Pennsylvania Press.

LACAN, F. (1975), *The Language of the Self*, Delta, New York.

LACAN, F. (1977a), *Ecrits*, London, Tavistock.

LACAN, F. (1977b), 'Preface by Jacques Lacan' in Lemaire (1977).

LACLAU, E. (1975), 'The Specificity of the Political', *Economy and Society* 4 (1).

LAKATOS, I. (1970), 'Falsification and the Methodology of Scientific Research Programmes', in Lakatos, I. and Musgrave, A. (1970), *Criticism and the Growth of Knowledge*, Cambridge University Press.

LEMAIRE, A. (1977), *Jacques Lacan*, London, Routledge & Kegan Paul.

LENIN, V. (1947), '*State and Revolution*' in *Selected Works*, London, Lawrence & Wishart.

LLOYD, E. (1972), *Introduction to Jurisprudence*, London, Stevens.

McCABE, C., in Barker, F. *et al.* (1977), *Literature, Society and the Sociology of Literature* (Proceedings of 1976 Conference), Essex Sociology of Literature Publishing Corporation, Essex.

MACKSEY, R. and DONATO, E. (1972), *The Language of Criticism and The Science of Man*, London, Johns Hopkins Press.

McLENNAN, G. (1978), 'Correspondence', *Economy and Society*, 7, (2): 193–205.

MARX, K. (1967), *Capital*, vol. I, London, Lawrence & Wishart.

MARX, K. and ENGELS, F. (1969), *The German Ideology*, London, Lawrence & Wishart.

MEAD, G. H. (1934), *Mind, Self and Society*, University of Chicago Press.

MÜLLER, W. and NEUSÜSS, C. (1978), 'The "Welfare State Illusion" and the Contradiction between Wage Labour and Capital', in Holloway and Picciotto (1978).

MITCHELL, J. (1974), *Psychoanalysis and Feminism*, London, Allen Lane.

MUNGHAM, G. and BANKOWSKI, Z. (1977), The Jury in the Legal System in Carlen, P. *Sociological Review Monograph on the Sociology of Law*.

PAREKH, B. (1974), *Jeremy Bentham*, London, Frank Cass.

PARSONS, T. (1937), *The Structure of Social Action*, New York, McGraw Hill.

PASHUKANIS, E. (1951), General Theory of Law and Marxism, in *Soviet Legal Philosophy*, V. I. Lenin *et al.* (trans. H. Babb) *Twentieth Century Legal Philosophy Series No. 5*, Harvard University Press (reprinted 1968. Johnson Reprint Company).

PEMBERTON, J. (1973), *British Official Publications*, Oxford, Pergamon.

PITKIN, H. (1972), *Wittgenstein and Justice*, University of California Press.

POPPER, K. (1972), *Objective Knowledge*, Oxford University Press.

POPPER, K. (1974), in P. Schilp (ed.) *The Philosophy of Karl Popper*, New York, Open Court.

POULANTZAS, N. (1975a), *Political Power and Social Classes*, London, New Left Books.

POULANTZAS, N. (1975b), *Classes in Contemporary Capitalism*, London, New Left Books.

POULANTZAS, N. (1976), Controversy Over the State, *New Left Review* 95, February.

PRATT, M. L. (1977), *Toward a Speech Act Theory of Discourse*, Bloomington, University of Indiana Press.

RAWLS, J. (1955), 'Two Concepts of Rules', *Philosophical Review* 64.

RAWLS, J. (1972), *Theory of Justice*, London, Oxford University Press.

SACHS, A. (1976), 'The Myth of Judicial Neutrality' in Carlen (1976).

SAUSSURE, F. (1974), *Course in General Linguistics*, London, Fontana.

SCARMAN, LORD (1976), *Guardian*, 1 March.

SEARLE, J. (1971), *The Philosophy of Language*, Oxford University Press.

SEBEOK, T. (1975), *The Tell-Tale Sign*, Peter de Ridder Press.

SOLLERS, P. (1974), *Sur le matérialisme*, Editions du Seuil, Paris.

SPICER, R. (1976), 'Conspiracy Law, Class and Society' in Carlen 1976.

STALIN, J. (1973), *The Essential Stalin* (ed. Bruce Franklin), London, Croom-Helm.

STONE, J. (1964), *Legal System and Lawyers' Reasoning*, London, Stevens & Sons.

SUTHERLAND, G. (ed.) (1969), *Studies in the Growth of Nineteenth Century Government*, London, Routledge & Kegan Paul.

TIMPANARO, S. (1975), *On Materialism*, London, New Left Books.

TWINING, W. and MIERS (1976), *How to Do Things With Rules*, London, Weidenfeld & Nicolson.

VOLOSINOV, V. (1973), *Marxism and The Philosophy of Language*, London, Academic Press.

VOLOSINOV, V. (1976), *Freudianism: A Marxist Critique*, London, Academic Press.

WHORF, B. (1952), *Language, Thought and Reality*, Massachusetts Institute of Technology.

WILDEN, A. (1972), *System and Structure*, London, Tavistock.

WILDEN, A. (1975), Introduction to Lacan J. *The Language of The Self*, New York, Delta.

WILLIAMS, K. (1975), 'Facing Reality: A Critique of Popper's Empiricism'. *Economy and Society*, 5 (3).

WILLIAMS, R. (1978), 'Timpanaro's Materialist Challenge', *New Left Review*, 109: 3–17.

WITTGENSTEIN, L. (1964), *The Blue and Brown Books*, New York, Harper & Row.

Index

145

Routledge Social Science Series

Routledge & Kegan Paul   London, Henley and Boston

39 Store Street, London WC1E 7DD
Broadway House, Newtown Road,
Henley-on-Thames, Oxon RG9 1EN
9 Park Street, Boston, Mass. 02108

Contents

*Authors wishing to submit manuscripts for any series in
this catalogue should send them to the Social Science Editor,
Routledge & Kegan Paul Ltd, 39 Store Street,
London WC1E 7DD*

● *Books so marked are available in paperback*
All books are in Metric Demy 8vo format (216 × 138mm approx.)

International Library of Sociology

General Editor   John Rex

GENERAL SOCIOLOGY

Barnsley, J. H. The Social Reality of Ethics. *464 pp.*
Brown, Robert. Explanation in Social Science. *208 pp.*
● Rules and Laws in Sociology. *192 pp.*
Bruford, W. H. Chekhov and His Russia. *A Sociological Study. 244 pp.*
Burton, F. and **Carlen, P.** Official Discourse. *On Discourse Analysis, Government Publications, Ideology. About 140 pp.*
Cain, Maureen E. Society and the Policeman's Role. *326 pp.*
●**Fletcher, Colin.** Beneath the Surface. *An Account of Three Styles of Sociological Research. 221 pp.*
Gibson, Quentin. The Logic of Social Enquiry. *240 pp.*
Glucksmann, M. Structuralist Analysis in Contemporary Social Thought. *212 pp.*
Gurvitch, Georges. Sociology of Law. *Foreword by Roscoe Pound. 264 pp.*
Hinkle, R. Founding Theory of American Sociology 1883-1915. *About 350 pp.*
Homans, George C. Sentiments and Activities. *336 pp.*
Johnson, Harry M. Sociology: *a Systematic Introduction. Foreword by Robert K. Merton. 710 pp.*
● **Keat, Russell** and **Urry, John.** Social Theory as Science. *278 pp.*
Mannheim, Karl. Essays on Sociology and Social Psychology. *Edited by Paul Keckskemeti. With Editorial Note by Adolph Lowe. 344 pp.*
Martindale, Don. The Nature and Types of Sociological Theory. *292 pp.*
●**Maus, Heinz.** A Short History of Sociology. *234 pp.*
Myrdal, Gunnar. Value in Social Theory: *A Collection of Essays on Methodology. Edited by Paul Streeten. 332 pp.*
Ogburn, William F. and **Nimkoff, Meyer F.** A Handbook of Sociology. *Preface by Karl Mannheim. 656 pp. 46 figures. 35 tables.*
Parsons, Talcott, and **Smelser, Neil J.** Economy and Society: *A Study in the Integration of Economic and Social Theory. 362 pp.*
Podgórecki, Adam. Practical Social Sciences. *About 200 pp.*
Raffel, S. Matters of Fact. *A Sociological Inquiry. 152 pp.*
● **Rex, John.** (Ed.) Approaches to Sociology. *Contributions by Peter Abell,* Sociology and the Demystification of the Modern World. *282 pp.*
●**Rex, John** (Ed.) Approaches to Sociology. *Contributions by Peter Abell, Frank Bechhofer, Basil Bernstein, Ronald Fletcher, David Frisby, Miriam Glucksmann, Peter Lassman, Herminio Martins, John Rex, Roland Robertson, John Westergaard and Jock Young. 302 pp.*
Rigby, A. Alternative Realities. *352 pp.*
Roche, M. Phenomenology, Language and the Social Sciences. *374 pp.*
Sahay, A. Sociological Analysis. *220 pp.*

Strasser, Hermann. The Normative Structure of Sociology. *Conservative and Emancipatory Themes in Social Thought. About 340 pp.*
Strong, P. Ceremonial Order of the Clinic. *About 250 pp.*
Urry, John. Reference Groups and the Theory of Revolution. *244 pp.*
Weinberg, E. Development of Sociology in the Soviet Union. *173 pp.*

FOREIGN CLASSICS OF SOCIOLOGY

● **Gerth, H. H.** and **Mills, C. Wright.** From Max Weber: *Essays in Sociology. 502 pp.*
● **Tönnies, Ferdinand.** Community and Association. *(Gemeinschaft and Gesellschaft.) Translated and Supplemented by Charles P. Loomis. Foreword by Pitirim A. Sorokin. 334 pp.*

SOCIAL STRUCTURE

Andreski, Stanislav. Military Organization and Society. *Foreword by Professor A. R. Radcliffe-Brown. 226 pp. 1 folder.*
Carlton, Eric. Ideology and Social Order. *Foreword by Professor Philip Abrahams. About 320 pp.*
Coontz, Sydney H. Population Theories and the Economic Interpretation. *202 pp.*
Coser, Lewis. The Functions of Social Conflict. *204 pp.*
Dickie-Clark, H. F. Marginal Situation: *A Sociological Study of a Coloured Group. 240 pp. 11 tables.*
Giner, S. and **Archer, M. S.** (Eds.). Contemporary Europe. *Social Structures and Cultural Patterns. 336 pp.*
● **Glaser, Barney** and **Strauss, Anselm L.** Status Passage. *A Formal Theory. 212 pp.*
Glass, D. V. (Ed.) Social Mobility in Britain. *Contributions by J. Berent, T. Bottomore, R. C. Chambers, J. Floud, D. V. Glass, J. R. Hall, H. T. Himmelweit, R. K. Kelsall, F. M. Martin, C. A. Moser, R. Mukherjee, and W. Ziegel. 420 pp.*
Kelsall, R. K. Higher Civil Servants in Britain: *From 1870 to the Present Day. 268 pp. 31 tables.*
● **Lawton, Denis.** Social Class, Language and Education. *192 pp.*
McLeish, John. The Theory of Social Change: *Four Views Considered. 128 pp.*
● **Marsh, David C.** The Changing Social Structure of England and Wales, 1871-1961. *Revised edition. 288 pp.*
Menzies, Ken. Talcott Parsons and the Social Image of Man. *About 208 pp.*
● **Mouzelis, Nicos.** Organization and Bureaucracy. *An Analysis of Modern Theories. 240 pp.*
Ossowski, Stanislaw. Class Structure in the Social Consciousness. *210 pp.*
● **Podgórecki, Adam.** Law and Society. *302 pp.*
Renner, Karl. Institutions of Private Law and Their Social Functions. *Edited, with an Introduction and Notes, by O. Kahn-Freud. Translated by Agnes Schwarzschild. 316 pp.*

Rex, J. and **Tomlinson, S.** Colonial Immigrants in a British City. *A Class Analysis. 368 pp.*

Smooha, S. Israel: Pluralism and Conflict. *472 pp.*

Wesolowski, W. Class, Strata and Power. *Trans. and with Introduction by G. Kolankiewicz. 160 pp.*

Zureik, E. Palestinians in Israel. *A Study in Internal Colonialism. 264 pp.*

SOCIOLOGY AND POLITICS

Acton, T. A. Gypsy Politics and Social Change. *316 pp.*

Burton, F. Politics of Legitimacy. *Struggles in a Belfast Community. 250 pp.*

Etzioni-Halevy, E. Political Manipulation and Administrative Power. *A Comparative Study. About 200 pp.*

● **Hechter, Michael.** Internal Colonialism. *The Celtic Fringe in British National Development, 1536–1966. 380 pp.*

Kornhauser, William. The Politics of Mass Society. *272 pp. 20 tables.*

Korpi, W. The Working Class in Welfare Capitalism. *Work, Unions and Politics in Sweden. 472 pp.*

Kroes, R. Soldiers and Students. *A Study of Right- and Left-wing Students. 174 pp.*

Martin, Roderick. Sociology of Power. *About 272 pp.*

Myrdal, Gunnar. The Political Element in the Development of Economic Theory. *Translated from the German by Paul Streeten. 282 pp.*

Wong, S.-L. Sociology and Socialism in Contemporary China. *160 pp.*

Wootton, Graham. Workers, Unions and the State. *188 pp.*

CRIMINOLOGY

Ancel, Marc. Social Defence: *A Modern Approach to Criminal Problems. Foreword by Leon Radzinowicz. 240 pp.*

Athens, L. Violent Criminal Acts and Actors. *About 150 pp.*

Cain, Maureen E. Society and the Policeman's Role. *326 pp.*

Cloward, Richard A. and **Ohlin, Lloyd E.** Delinquency and Opportunity: *A Theory of Delinquent Gangs. 248 pp.*

Downes, David M. The Delinquent Solution. *A Study in Subcultural Theory. 296 pp.*

Friedlander, Kate. The Psycho-Analytical Approach to Juvenile Delinquency: *Theory, Case Studies, Treatment. 320 pp.*

Gleuck, Sheldon and **Eleanor.** Family Environment and Delinquency. *With the statistical assistance of Rose W. Kneznek. 340 pp.*

Lopez-Rey, Manuel. Crime. *An Analytical Appraisal. 288 pp.*

Mannheim, Hermann. Comparative Criminology: *a Text Book. Two volumes. 442 pp. and 380 pp.*

Morris, Terence. The Criminal Area: *A Study in Social Ecology. Foreword by Hermann Mannheim. 232 pp. 25 tables. 4 maps.*

Podgorecki, A. and **Łos, M.** *Multidimensional Sociology. About 380 pp.*

Rock, Paul. Making People Pay. *338 pp.*

● **Taylor, Ian, Walton, Paul,** and **Young, Jock.** The New Criminology. *For a Social Theory of Deviance. 325 pp.*
● **Taylor, Ian, Walton, Paul** and **Young, Jock.** (Eds) Critical Criminology. *268 pp.*

SOCIAL PSYCHOLOGY

Bagley, Christopher. The Social Psychology of the Epileptic Child. *320 pp.*
Brittan, Arthur. Meanings and Situations. *224 pp.*
Carroll, J. Break-Out from the Crystal Palace. *200 pp.*
● **Fleming, C. M.** Adolescence: Its Social Psychology. *With an Introduction to recent findings from the fields of Anthropology, Physiology, Medicine, Psychometrics and Sociometry. 288 pp.*
● The Social Psychology of Education: *An Introduction and Guide to Its Study. 136 pp.*
Linton, Ralph. The Cultural Background of Personality. *132 pp.*
● **Mayo, Elton.** The Social Problems of an Industrial Civilization. *With an Appendix on the Political Problem. 180 pp.*
Ottaway, A. K. C. Learning Through Group Experience. *176 pp.*
Plummer, Ken. Sexual Stigma. *An Interactionist Account. 254 pp.*
● **Rose, Arnold M.** (Ed.) Human Behaviour and Social Processes: *an Interactionist Approach. Contributions by Arnold M. Rose, Ralph H. Turner, Anselm Strauss, Everett C. Hughes, E. Franklin Frazier, Howard S. Becker et al. 696 pp.*
Smelser, Neil J. Theory of Collective Behaviour. *448 pp.*
Stephenson, Geoffrey M. The Development of Conscience. *128 pp.*
Young, Kimball. Handbook of Social Psychology. *658 pp. 16 figures. 10 tables.*

SOCIOLOGY OF THE FAMILY

Bell, Colin R. Middle Class Families: *Social and Geographical Mobility. 224 pp.*
Burton, Lindy. Vulnerable Children. *272 pp.*
Gavron, Hannah. The Captive Wife: *Conflicts of Household Mothers. 190 pp.*
George, Victor and **Wilding, Paul.** Motherless Families. *248 pp.*
Klein, Josephine. Samples from English Cultures.
　1. Three Preliminary Studies and Aspects of Adult Life in England. *447 pp.*
　2. Child-Rearing Practices and Index. *247 pp.*
Klein, Viola. The Feminine Character. *History of an Ideology. 244 pp.*
McWhinnie, Alexina M. Adopted Children. *How They Grow Up. 304 pp.*
● **Morgan, D. H. J.** Social Theory and the Family. *About 320 pp.*
● **Myrdal, Alva** and **Klein, Viola.** Women's Two Roles: *Home and Work. 238 pp. 27 tables.*

Parsons, Talcott and **Bales, Robert F.** Family: Socialization and Inter-
action Process. *In collaboration with James Olds, Morris Zelditch
and Philip E. Slater. 456 pp. 50 figures and tables.*

SOCIAL SERVICES

Bastide, Roger. The Sociology of Mental Disorder. *Translated from the
French by Jean McNeil. 260 pp.*

Carlebach, Julius. Caring For Children in Trouble. *266 pp.*

George, Victor. Foster Care. *Theory and Practice. 234 pp.*
Social Security: *Beveridge and After. 258 pp.*

George, V. and **Wilding, P.** Motherless Families. *248 pp.*

● **Goetschius, George W.** Working with Community Groups. *256 pp.*

Goetschius, George W. and **Tash, Joan.** Working with Unattached
Youth. *416 pp.*

Heywood, Jean S. Children in Care. *The Development of the Service for
the Deprived Child. Third revised edition. 284 pp.*

King, Roy D., Ranes, Norma V. and **Tizard, Jack.** Patterns of Residen-
tial Care. *356 pp.*

Leigh, John. Young People and Leisure. *256 pp.*

● **Mays, John.** (Ed.) Penelope Hall's Social Services of England and Wales.
About 324 pp.

Morris, Mary. Voluntary Work and the Welfare State. *300 pp.*

Nokes, P. L. The Professional Task in Welfare Practice. *152 pp.*

Timms, Noel. Psychiatric Social Work in Great Britain (1939-1962).
280 pp.

● Social Casework: *Principles and Practice. 256 pp.*

SOCIOLOGY OF EDUCATION

Banks, Olive. Parity and Prestige in English Secondary Education: a
Study in Educational Sociology. *272 pp.*

● **Blyth, W. A. L.** English Primary Education. *A Sociological Description.*
2. Background. *168 pp.*

Collier, K. G. The Social Purposes of Education: *Personal and Social
Values in Education. 268 pp.*

Evans, K. M. Sociometry and Education. *158 pp.*

● **Ford, Julienne.** Social Class and the Comprehensive School. *192 pp.*

Foster, P. J. Education and Social Change in Ghana. *336 pp. 3 maps.*

Fraser, W. R. Education and Society in Modern France. *150 pp.*

Grace, Gerald R. Role Conflict and the Teacher. *150 pp.*

Hans, Nicholas. New Trends in Education in the Eighteenth Century.
278 pp. 19 tables.

● Comparative Education: *A Study of Educational Factors and Tra-
ditions. 360 pp.*

● **Hargreaves, David.** Interpersonal Relations and Education. *432 pp.*

● Social Relations in a Secondary School. *240 pp.*

School Organization and Pupil Involvement. *A Study of Secondary
Schools.*

● **Mannheim, Karl** and **Stewart, W.A.C.** An Introduction to the Sociology of Education. *206 pp.*

● **Musgrove, F.** Youth and the Social Order. *176 pp.*

● **Ottaway, A. K. C.** Education and Society: An Introduction to the Sociology of Education. *With an Introduction by W. O. Lester Smith. 212 pp.*

Peers, Robert. Adult Education: *A Comparative Study. Revised edition. 398 pp.*

Stratta, Erica. The Education of Borstal Boys. *A Study of their Educational Experiences prior to, and during, Borstal Training. 256 pp.*

● **Taylor, P. H., Reid, W. A.** and **Holley, B. J.** The English Sixth Form. *A Case Study in Curriculum Research. 198 pp.*

SOCIOLOGY OF CULTURE

Eppel, E. M. and **M.** Adolescents and Morality: *A Study of some Moral Values and Dilemmas of Working Adolescents in the Context of a changing Climate of Opinion. Foreword by W. J. H. Sprott. 268 pp. 39 tables.*

● **Fromm, Erich.** The Fear of Freedom. *286 pp.*
●   The Sane Society. *400 pp.*

Johnson, L. The Cultural Critics. *From Matthew Arnold to Raymond Williams. 233 pp.*

Mannheim, Karl. Essays on the Sociology of Culture. *Edited by Ernst Mannheim in co-operation with Paul Kecskemeti. Editorial Note by Adolph Lowe. 280 pp.*

Zijderfeld, A. C. On Clichés. *The Supersedure of Meaning by Function in Modernity. About 132 pp.*

SOCIOLOGY OF RELIGION

Argyle, Michael and **Beit-Hallahmi, Benjamin.** The Social Psychology of Religion. *About 256 pp.*

Glasner, Peter E. The Sociology of Secularisation. *A Critique of a Concept. About 180 pp.*

Hall, J. R. The Ways Out. *Utopian Communal Groups in an Age of Babylon. 280 pp.*

Ranson, S., Hinings, B. and **Bryman, A.** Clergy, Ministers and Priests. *216 pp.*

Stark, Werner. The Sociology of Religion. *A Study of Christendom.*
    Volume II. *Sectarian Religion. 368 pp.*
    Volume III. *The Universal Church. 464 pp.*
    Volume IV. *Types of Religious Man. 352 pp.*
    Volume V. *Types of Religious Culture. 464 pp.*

Turner, B. S. Weber and Islam. *216 pp.*

Watt, W. Montgomery. Islam and the Integration of Society. *320 pp.*

SOCIOLOGY OF ART AND LITERATURE

Jarvie, Ian C. Towards a Sociology of the Cinema. *A Comparative Essay on the Structure and Functioning of a Major Entertainment Industry. 405 pp.*

Rust, Frances S. Dance in Society. *An Analysis of the Relationships between the Social Dance and Society in England from the Middle Ages to the Present Day. 256 pp. 8 pp. of plates.*

Schücking, L. L. The Sociology of Literary Taste. *112 pp.*

Wolff, Janet. Hermeneutic Philosophy and the Sociology of Art. *150 pp.*

SOCIOLOGY OF KNOWLEDGE

Diesing, P. Patterns of Discovery in the Social Sciences. *262 pp.*

● **Douglas, J. D.** (Ed.) Understanding Everyday Life. *370 pp.*

Glasner, B. Essential Interactionism. *About 220 pp.*

● **Hamilton, P.** Knowledge and Social Structure. *174 pp.*

Jarvie, I. C. Concepts and Society. *232 pp.*

Mannheim, Karl. Essays on the Sociology of Knowledge. *Edited by Paul Kecskemeti. Editorial Note by Adolph Lowe. 353 pp.*

Remmling, Gunter W. The Sociology of Karl Mannheim. *With a Bibliographical Guide to the Sociology of Knowledge, Ideological Analysis, and Social Planning. 255 pp.*

Remmling, Gunter W. (Ed.) Towards the Sociology of Knowledge. *Origin and Development of a Sociological Thought Style. 463 pp.*

URBAN SOCIOLOGY

Aldridge, M. The British New Towns. *A Programme Without a Policy. About 250 pp.*

Ashworth, William. The Genesis of Modern British Town Planning: *A Study in Economic and Social History of the Nineteenth and Twentieth Centuries. 288 pp.*

Brittan, A. The Privatised World. *196 pp.*

Cullingworth, J. B. Housing Needs and Planning Policy: *A Restatement of the Problems of Housing Need and 'Overspill' in England and Wales. 232 pp. 44 tables. 8 maps.*

Dickinson, Robert E. City and Region: *A Geographical Interpretation. 608 pp. 125 figures.*

The West European City: *A Geographical Interpretation. 600 pp. 129 maps. 29 plates.*

Humphreys, Alexander J. New Dubliners: *Urbanization and the Irish Family. Foreword by George C. Homans. 304 pp.*

Jackson, Brian. Working Class Community: *Some General Notions raised by a Series of Studies in Northern England. 192 pp.*

● **Mann, P. H.** An Approach to Urban Sociology. *240 pp.*

Mellor, J. R. Urban Sociology in an Urbanized Society. *326 pp.*

Morris, R. N. and **Mogey, J.** The Sociology of Housing. *Studies at Berinsfield. 232 pp. 4 pp. plates.*

Rosser, C. and **Harris, C.** The Family and Social Change. *A Study of Family and Kinship in a South Wales Town. 352 pp. 8 maps.*

● **Stacey, Margaret, Batsone, Eric, Bell, Colin** and **Thurcott, Anne.** Power, Persistence and Change. *A Second Study of Banbury. 196 pp.*

RURAL SOCIOLOGY

Mayer, Adrian C. Peasants in the Pacific. *A Study of Fiji Indian Rural Society. 248 pp. 20 plates.*

Williams, W. M. The Sociology of an English Village: *Gosforth. 272 pp. 12 figures. 13 tables.*

SOCIOLOGY OF INDUSTRY AND DISTRIBUTION

Dunkerley, David. The Foreman. *Aspects of Task and Structure. 192 pp.*

Eldridge, J. E. T. Industrial Disputes. *Essays in the Sociology of Industrial Relations. 288 pp.*

Hollowell, Peter G. The Lorry Driver. *272 pp.*

● **Oxaal, I., Barnett, T.** and **Booth, D.** (Eds) Beyond the Sociology of Development. *Economy and Society in Latin America and Africa. 295 pp.*

Smelser, Neil J. Social Change in the Industrial Revolution: *An Application of Theory to the Lancashire Cotton Industry, 1770–1840. 468 pp. 12 figures. 14 tables.*

Watson, T. J. The Personnel Managers. *A Study in the Sociology of Work and Employment. 262 pp.*

ANTHROPOLOGY

Brandel-Syrier, Mia. Reeftown Elite. *A Study of Social Mobility in a Modern African Community on the Reef. 376 pp.*

Dickie-Clark, H. F. The Marginal Situation. *A Sociological Study of a Coloured Group. 236 pp.*

Dube, S. C. Indian Village. *Foreword by Morris Edward Opler. 276 pp. 4 plates.*

India's Changing Villages: *Human Factors in Community Development. 260 pp. 8 plates. 1 map.*

Firth, Raymond. Malay Fishermen. *Their Peasant Economy. 420 pp. 17 pp. plates.*

Gulliver, P. H. Social Control in an African Society: a Study of the Arusha, Agricultural Masai of Northern Tanganyika. *320 pp. 8 plates. 10 figures.*

Family Herds. *288 pp.*

Jarvie, Ian C. The Revolution in Anthropology. *268 pp.*

Little, Kenneth L. Mende of Sierra Leone. *308 pp. and folder.*

Negroes in Britain. *With a New Introduction and Contemporary Study by Leonard Bloom. 320 pp.*

Madan, G. R. Western Sociologists on Indian Society. *Marx, Spencer, Weber, Durkheim, Pareto. 384 pp.*

Mayer, A. C. Peasants in the Pacific. *A Study of Fiji Indian Rural Society. 248 pp.*

Meer, Fatima. Race and Suicide in South Africa. *325 pp.*

Smith, Raymond T. The Negro Family in British Guiana: *Family Structure and Social Status in the Villages. With a Foreword by Meyer Fortes. 314 pp. 8 plates. 1 figure. 4 maps.*

SOCIOLOGY AND PHILOSOPHY

Barnsley, John H. The Social Reality of Ethics. *A Comparative Analysis of Moral Codes. 448 pp.*

Diesing, Paul. Patterns of Discovery in the Social Sciences. *362 pp.*

● **Douglas, Jack D.** (Ed.) Understanding Everyday Life. *Toward the Reconstruction of Sociological Knowledge. Contributions by Alan F. Blum, Aaron W. Cicourel, Norman K. Denzin, Jack D. Douglas, John Heeren, Peter McHugh, Peter K. Manning, Melvin Power, Matthew Speier, Roy Turner, D. Lawrence Wieder, Thomas P. Wilson and Don H. Zimmerman. 370 pp.*

Gorman, Robert A. The Dual Vision. *Alfred Schutz and the Myth of Phenomenological Social Science. About 300 pp.*

Jarvie, Ian C. Concepts and Society. *216 pp.*

Kilminster, R. Praxis and Method. *A Sociological Dialogue with Lukács, Gramsci and the early Frankfurt School. About 304 pp.*

● **Pelz, Werner.** The Scope of Understanding in Sociology. *Towards a More Radical Reorientation in the Social Humanistic Sciences. 283 pp.*

Roche, Maurice. Phenomenology, Language and the Social Sciences. *371 pp.*

Sahay, Arun. Sociological Analysis. *212 pp.*

Slater, P. Origin and Significance of the Frankfurt School. *A Marxist Perspective. About 192 pp.*

Spurling, L. Phenomenology and the Social World. *The Philosophy of Merleau-Ponty and its Relation to the Social Sciences. 222 pp.*

Wilson, H. T. The American Ideology. *Science, Technology and Organization as Modes of Rationality. 368 pp.*

International Library of Anthropology

General Editor Adam Kuper

Ahmed, A. S. Millenium and Charisma Among Pathans. *A Critical Essay in Social Anthropology. 192 pp.*
Pukhtun Economy and Society. *About 360 pp.*

Brown, Paula. The Chimbu. *A Study of Change in the New Guinea Highlands. 151 pp.*

Foner, N. Jamaica Farewell. *200 pp.*

Gudeman, Stephen. Relationships, Residence and the Individual. *A Rural Panamanian Community. 288 pp. 11 plates, 5 figures, 2 maps, 10 tables.*
The Demise of a Rural Economy. *From Subsistence to Capitalism in a Latin American Village. 160 pp.*

Hamnett, Ian. Chieftainship and Legitimacy. *An Anthropological Study of Executive Law in Lesotho. 163 pp.*

Hanson, F. Allan. Meaning in Culture. *127 pp.*

Humphreys, S. C. Anthropology and the Greeks. *288 pp.*

Karp, I. Fields of Change Among the Iteso of Kenya. *140 pp.*

Lloyd, P. C. Power and Independence. *Urban Africans' Perception of Social Inequality. 264 pp.*

Parry, J. P. Caste and Kinship in Kangra. *352 pp. Illustrated.*

Pettigrew, Joyce. Robber Noblemen. *A Study of the Political System of the Sikh Jats. 284 pp.*

Street, Brian V. The Savage in Literature. *Representations of 'Primitive' Society in English Fiction, 1858–1920. 207 pp.*

Van Den Berghe, Pierre L. Power and Privilege at an African University. *278 pp.*

International Library of Social Policy

General Editor Kathleen Jones

Bayley, M. Mental Handicap and Community Care. *426 pp.*

Bottoms, A. E. and **McClean, J. D.** Defendants in the Criminal Process. *284 pp.*

Butler, J. R. Family Doctors and Public Policy. *208 pp.*

Davies, Martin. Prisoners of Society. *Attitudes and Aftercare. 204 pp.*

Gittus, Elizabeth. Flats, Families and the Under-Fives. *285 pp.*

Holman, Robert. Trading in Children. *A Study of Private Fostering. 355 pp.*

Jeffs, A. Young People and the Youth Service. *About 180 pp.*

Jones, Howard, and **Cornes, Paul.** Open Prisons. *288 pp.*

Jones, Kathleen. History of the Mental Health Service. *428 pp.*

Jones, Kathleen, with **Brown, John, Cunningham, W. J., Roberts, Julian** and **Williams, Peter.** Opening the Door. *A Study of New Policies for the Mentally Handicapped. 278 pp.*

Karn, Valerie. Retiring to the Seaside. *About 280 pp. 2 maps. Numerous tables.*

King, R. D. and **Elliot, K. W.** Albany: Birth of a Prison—End of an Era. *394 pp.*

Thomas, J. E. The English Prison Officer since 1850: *A Study in Conflict. 258 pp.*

Walton, R. G. Women in Social Work. *303 pp.*

● **Woodward, J.** To Do the Sick No Harm. *A Study of the British Voluntary Hospital System to 1875. 234 pp.*

International Library of Welfare and Philosophy

General Editors Noel Timms and David Watson

● **McDermott, F. E.** (Ed.) Self-Determination in Social Work. *A Collection of Essays on Self-determination and Related Concepts by Philosophers and Social Work Theorists. Contributors: F. B. Biestek, S. Bernstein, A. Keith-Lucas, D. Sayer, H. H. Perelman, C. Whittington, R. F. Stalley, F. E. McDermott, I. Berlin, H. J. McCloskey, H. L. A. Hart, J. Wilson, A. I. Melden, S. I. Benn. 254 pp.*

● **Plant, Raymond.** Community and Ideology. *104 pp.*

Ragg, Nicholas M. People Not Cases. *A Philosophical Approach to Social Work. About 250 pp.*

● **Timms, Noel** and **Watson, David.** (Eds) Talking About Welfare. *Readings in Philosophy and Social Policy. Contributors: T. H. Marshall, R. B. Brandt, G. H. von Wright, K. Nielsen, M. Cranston, R. M. Titmuss, R. S. Downie, E. Telfer, D. Donnison, J. Benson, P. Leonard, A. Keith-Lucas, D. Walsh, I. T. Ramsey. 320 pp.*

● (Eds). Philosophy in Social Work. *250 pp.*

● **Weale, A.** Equality and Social Policy. *164 pp.*

Primary Socialization, Language and Education

General Editor Basil Bernstein

Adlam, Diana S., *with the assistance of Geoffrey Turner and Lesley Lineker.* Code in Context. *About 272 pp.*

Bernstein, Basil. Class, Codes and Control. *3 volumes.*

● 1. *Theoretical Studies Towards a Sociology of Language. 254 pp.*

2. *Applied Studies Towards a Sociology of Language. 377 pp.*

● 3. *Towards a Theory of Educational Transmission. 167 pp.*

Brandis, W. and **Bernstein, B.** Selection and Control. *176 pp.*

Brandis, Walter and **Henderson, Dorothy.** Social Class, Language and Communication. *288 pp.*

Cook-Gumperz, Jenny. Social Control and Socialization. *A Study of Class Differences in the Language of Maternal Control. 290 pp.*

● **Gahagan, D. M** and **G. A.** Talk Reform. *Exploration in Language for Infant School Children. 160 pp.*

Hawkins, P. R. Social Class, the Nominal Group and Verbal Strategies. *About 220 pp.*

Robinson, W. P. and **Rackstraw, Susan D. A.** A Question of Answers. *2 volumes. 192 pp. and 180 pp.*

Turner, Geoffrey J. and **Mohan, Bernard A.** A Linguistic Description and Computer Programme for Children's Speech. *208 pp.*

Reports of the Institute of Community Studies

Baker, J. The Neighbourhood Advice Centre. A Community Project in Camden. *320 pp.*

● **Cartwright, Ann.** Patients and their Doctors. *A Study of General Practice. 304 pp.*

Dench, Geoff. Maltese in London. *A Case-study in the Erosion of Ethnic Consciousness. 302 pp.*

Jackson, Brian and **Marsden, Dennis.** Education and the Working Class: *Some General Themes raised by a Study of 88 Working-class Children in a Northern Industrial City. 268 pp. 2 folders.*

Marris, Peter. The Experience of Higher Education. *232 pp. 27 tables.*

● Loss and Change. *192 pp.*

Marris, Peter and **Rein, Martin.** Dilemmas of Social Reform. *Poverty and Community Action in the United States. 256 pp.*

Marris, Peter and **Somerset, Anthony.** African Businessmen. *A Study of Entrepreneurship and Development in Keyna. 256 pp.*

Mills, Richard. Young Outsiders: *a Study in Alternative Communities. 216 pp.*

Runciman, W. G. Relative Deprivation and Social Justice. *A Study of Attitudes to Social Inequality in Twentieth-Century England. 352 pp.*

Willmott, Peter. Adolescent Boys in East London. *230 pp.*

Willmott, Peter and **Young, Michael.** Family and Class in a London Suburb. *202 pp. 47 tables.*

Young, Michael and **McGeeney, Patrick.** Learning Begins at Home. *A Study of a Junior School and its Parents. 128 pp.*

Young, Michael and **Willmott, Peter.** Family and Kinship in East London. *Foreword by Richard M. Titmuss. 252 pp. 39 tables.*

The Symmetrical Family. *410 pp.*

Reports of the Institute for Social Studies in Medical Care

Cartwright, Ann, Hockey, Lisbeth and **Anderson, John J.** Life Before Death. *310 pp.*

Dunnell, Karen and **Cartwright, Ann.** Medicine Takers, Prescribers and Hoarders. *190 pp.*

Farrell, C. My Mother Said. . . . *A Study of the Way Young People Learned About Sex and Birth Control. 200 pp.*

Medicine, Illness and Society

General Editor   W. M. Williams

Hall, David J. Social Relations & Innovation. *Changing the State of Play in Hospitals. 232 pp.*

Hall, David J., and **Stacey, M.** (Eds) Beyond Separation. *234 pp.*

Robinson, David. The Process of Becoming Ill. *142 pp.*

Stacey, Margaret *et al.* Hospitals, Children and Their Families. *The Report of a Pilot Study. 202 pp.*

Stimson G. V. and **Webb, B.** Going to See the Doctor. *The Consultation Process in General Practice. 155 pp.*

Monographs in Social Theory

General Editor   Arthur Brittan

● **Barnes, B.** Scientific Knowledge and Sociological Theory. *192 pp.*

Bauman, Zygmunt. Culture as Praxis. *204 pp.*

● **Dixon, Keith.** Sociological Theory. *Pretence and Possibility. 142 pp.*

Meltzer, B. N., Petras, J. W. and **Reynolds, L. T.** Symbolic Interactionism. *Genesis, Varieties and Criticisms. 144 pp.*

● **Smith, Anthony D.** The Concept of Social Change. *A Critique of the Functionalist Theory of Social Change. 208 pp.*

Routledge Social Science Journals

The British Journal of Sociology. *Editor – Angus Stewart; Associate Editor – Leslie Sklair. Vol. 1, No. 1 – March 1950 and Quarterly. Roy. 8vo. All back issues available. An international journal publishing original papers in the field of sociology and related areas.*

Community Work. *Edited by David Jones and Marjorie Mayo. 1973. Published annually.*

Economy and Society. *Vol. 1, No. 1. February 1972 and Quarterly. Metric Roy. 8vo. A journal for all social scientists covering sociology, philosophy, anthropology, economics and history. All back numbers available.*

Ethnic and Racial Studies. *Editor – John Stone. Vol. 1 – 1978. Published quarterly.*

Religion. Journal of Religion and Religions. *Chairman of Editorial Board, Ninian Smart. Vol. 1, No. 1, Spring 1971. A journal with an interdisciplinary approach to the study of the phenomena of religion. All back numbers available.*

Sociology of Health and Illness. *A Journal of Medical Sociology. Editor – Alan Davies; Associate Editor – Ray Jobling. Vol. 1, Spring 1979. Published 3 times per annum.*

Year Book of Social Policy in Britain, The. *Edited by Kathleen Jones. 1971. Published annually.*

Social and Psychological Aspects of Medical Practice

Editor Trevor Silverstone

Lader, Malcolm. Psychophysiology of Mental Illness. *280 pp.*

● **Silverstone, Trevor** and **Turner, Paul.** Drug Treatment in Psychiatry. *Revised edition. 256 pp.*

Whiteley, J. S. and **Gordon, J.** Group Approaches in Psychiatry. *256 pp.*

Printed in Great Britain by
Lowe & Brydone Printers Limited, Thetford, Norfolk